'The world now stands on the brink of the final abyss. Let us all resolve to take all possible practical steps to ensure that we do not, through our own folly, go over the edge.'

Earl Mountbatten, 1979

ALSO BY JAMES AVERY JOYCE

World in the Making
Revolution on East River
World of Promise
Decade of Development
Capital Punishment: A World View
The Story of International Co-operation
Labour Faces the New Age
Jobs Versus People
The New Politics of Human Rights
World Labour Rights and their Protection
End of an Illusion
Justice at Work
Red Cross International
Broken Star: Story of the League of Nations
World Organization (symposium)
Human Rights: Basic Documents
World Population: Basic Documents

The War Machine

The Case against the Arms Race

James Avery Joyce

Quartet Books

London Melbourne New York

First published by Quartet Books Limited 1980
A member of the Namara Group
27/29 Goodge Street, London W1P 1FD

Copyright © 1980 by James Avery Joyce

ISBN 0 7043 2254 4

W 14394 £6.95. 1.81

Phototypeset by BSC Typesetting Ltd, London
Printed in Great Britain by litho at
The Anchor Press Ltd and bound by Wm Brendon Ltd,
both of Tiptree, Essex

Contents

Acknowledgments

The American side of our data owes much to the research data published by the Center for Defense Information in Washington, and I express my deep appreciation for the generous services extended to me by its Director, Rear-Admiral Gene R. La Rocque (US Navy, Ret.), and his indefatigable assistant, who received me so warmly in the Washington office. The aerospace and aeronautical data from the Smithsonian Institution relating to missiles and their vehicles has also proved invaluable. The State Department's regular bulletins were indispensable as a source of official data and statements of policy. In New York I have benefited especially from the careful researches of Professor Betty Lall of Cornell University and from Ruth Leger Sivard's annual survey of military expenditures. Studies and reports of the International Peace Academy, under the direction of Major-General Indar Jit Rikkye (Indian Army, Ret.) were most helpful in preparing my later chapters.

Among British sources, I found Dr John Cox's *Overkill* a *vade mecum* on nuclear weapons, and acknowledge my indebtedness to the author and publishers, Penguin Books Ltd. The reports of the Swedish International Peace Research Institute (SIPRI) provide the foundations for the sections devoted to the arms race, and I am indebted to the Institute and Josef Goldblat for permission to reprint their survey of multilateral arms agreements as Appendix (A).

In Geneva, practical help and advice came from many quarters including Mr Arthur Booth, Chairman of the International Peace Bureau (for reports of the 1977 Hiroshima seminar on radiation effects), and Mrs L. Waldheim-Natural, Chief of the Disarmament Centre at Le Palais des Nations, and her staff. Mr René Wadlow, Geneva representative of the Association of World Federalists has always been ready to supply me with just the data I needed.

For 30 years, the UN has published a considerable range of expert reports, not least the pamphlets and brochures published by its Department of Public Information, covering every possible aspect of the arms race and disarmament. These reports have been indispensable. Mrs Filiz Ertan, documentalist at the Geneva Centre, helped me prepare the important list of Further Reading at the end of this work.

From the wide variety of literature produced by non-governmental organizations for the UN Special Session on Disarmament, I have selected much that is not yet available in more substantial publications. I have also drawn considerably on the monthly editions of *Disarmament News*, under the editorship of Richard Hudson, whose *War/Peace Report* has for years been a goldmine of facts and figures.

Harry Robertson, Secretary of Labour Action for Peace, in London, provided me with up-to-date material, particularly on UK trade union activities, and he has checked some of the data that I have selected to support my proposals on British policy. Ronald Huzzard's bi-monthly *Labour Peace Newsletter* is cited many times; as are several publications of the redoubtable Campaign for Nuclear Disarmament (CND) and the Campaign Against the Arms Trade. *Sense about Defence* (Quartet Books, 1977), being a report of the Labour Party Defence Study Group, was most useful on questions of conversion. Other books and pamphlets cited are acknowledged in the references.

The maps and charts available at the Imperial War Museum have been most useful.

I also wish to thank the publishers, Sidgwick and Jackson, for permission to reproduce the map 'The Soviet Plan to attack Western Europe' from General Hackett's book *Third World War, August 1985*.

In admiration and respect for
Lt-General Ensio Siilasvuo
of Finland
former co-ordinator of
United Nations peace forces
in Jerusalem and
the Middle East

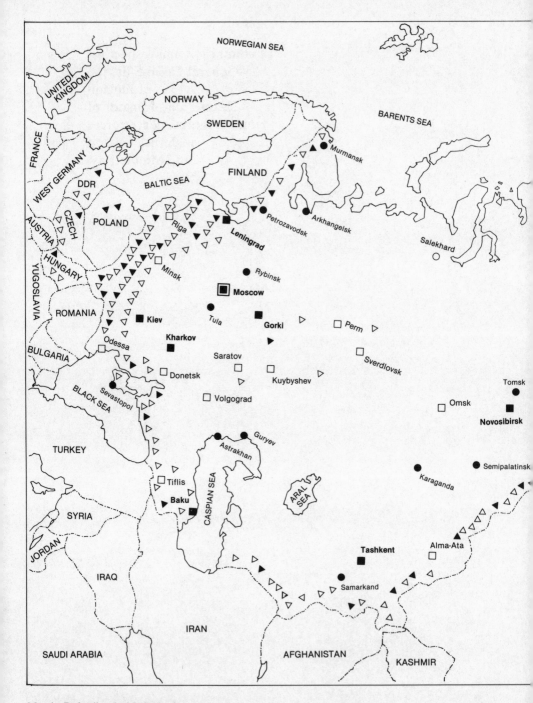

Map 1   Defending the Motherlands
Source: Phoebus Publishing Co/BPC Publishing Ltd 1975

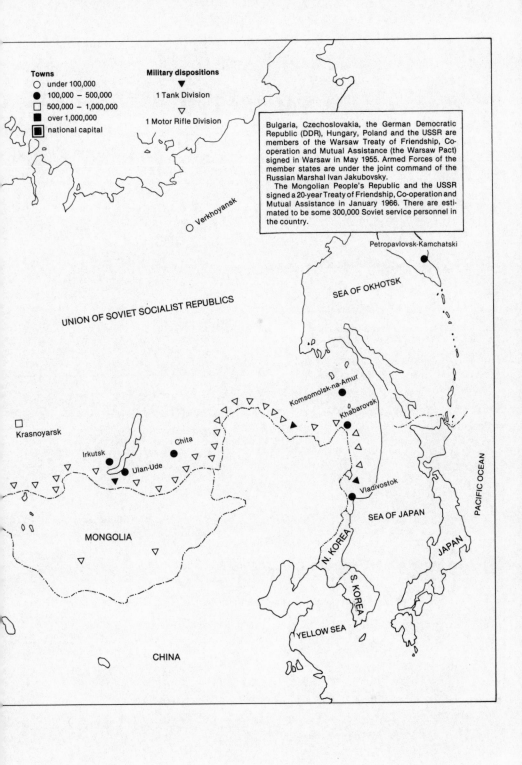

Towns
○ under 100,000
● 100,000 – 500,000
□ 500,000 – 1,000,000
■ over 1,000,000
▣ national capital

Military dispositions
▼ 1 Tank Division
▽ 1 Motor Rifle Division

Bulgaria, Czechoslovakia, the German Democratic Republic (DDR), Hungary, Poland and the USSR are members of the Warsaw Treaty of Friendship, Co-operation and Mutual Assistance (the Warsaw Pact) signed in Warsaw in May 1955. Armed Forces of the member states are under the joint command of the Russian Marshal Ivan Jakubovsky.

The Mongolian People's Republic and the USSR signed a 20-year Treaty of Friendship, Co-operation and Mutual Assistance in January 1966. There are estimated to be some 300,000 Soviet service personnel in the country.

○ Verkhoyansk

Petropavlovsk-Kamchatski

SEA OF OKHOTSK

UNION OF SOVIET SOCIALIST REPUBLICS

Komsomolsk-na-Amur

Khabarovsk

□ Krasnoyarsk

Chita

Irkutsk

Ulan-Ude

Vladivostok

PACIFIC OCEAN

SEA OF JAPAN

MONGOLIA

N. KOREA

S. KOREA

JAPAN

CHINA

YELLOW SEA

Introduction

This book is full of politics – the politics of survival, the politics of peace. But sometimes individual judgment in politics may err. This book can be no exception. Perhaps we shall overstate our case against the promoters of the arms race; perhaps we shall overlook the pressures of *realpolitik* on political decision makers; perhaps we shall over-estimate the conservatism of the powers-that-be; perhaps we shall under-estimate the impact of the press or the emotional reaction of the crowd that pushes them on or holds them back. But of two things in this arms business we are certain: that the ordinary people of this planet want and need peace, and their national politicians believe, with few exceptions, that they are providing it – in their own way. Yet, what must by now be as plain as daylight to increasing numbers of thinking people in all countries is that the arms race is *not* the way to get it. The arms race is a non-winner; it is a blind alley with a holocaust at the end of it.

Carl von Clausewitz, the great strategist, said: 'No human affair stands so constantly and so generally in close connection with chance as War.' Of all the branches of human activity, he added, war was 'the most like a gambling game'. That is why we cannot dodge examining political attitudes when we expose and condemn, as we do in these pages, the lies and shams and mis-conceptions in this gigantic balance of error that the arms race has become today. For the arms race is not basically about guns

1

or strategy or money; it is about political attitudes. It has been spawned by a military contest between the United States and the Soviet Union, and their respective allies and satellites. Though both sides talk about national security, the contest is really about military superiority – not equality but *superiority*.

The pro-Western press had for over a year been fed by Pentagon stories of the Soviet 'build-up' of tanks in Eastern Europe; but a study of the new Trident submarine with its 100 kilotons of explosive power aimed at 408 separate targets (which we describe in this book) leaves no doubt whatsoever that the US aims at overwhelming superiority. 'Equality' has lost any meaning today. A balance of terror turns out to be merely the politician's slapstick in a tragi-comedy of errors.

There are lesser aspects to be considered, of course – since there are many lesser armed struggles going on – but the United States and the Soviet Union's military rivalry is primary. We shall never lose sight of that; not even when we seek to explain, towards the end of this book, that the only viable solutions to this insane rivalry lie outside the areas of conflict altogether, namely, within the whole world community, acting through the United Nations system. For was not the UN Charter set up (as it says): 'to save succeeding generations from the scourge of war' and 'to practise tolerance and live together in peace with one another as good neighbours'?

Having started in 1945 from that common pledge to live and let live, how did we ever get onto this dreadful treadmill to oblivion? The fear of being 'out-manoeuvred' by the Soviet Union has so long dominated the minds of political leaders in the West that normal people have been seduced into believing that it can go on and on like this. But, as we enter the 1980s, we are living on borrowed time. Scientists, calculating the mathematical risks of the unthinkable happening, while megatons are being piled on megatons of mass-murder, spread across five continents, know that our days are getting close to zero.

Someone, sooner rather than later, will pull the wrong trigger, press the wrong button on this man-made inferno. Or someone will bump by accident into this monstrous network of military make-believe. The day before Armistice Day, 1979, we were six minutes away from a nuclear war, when the United States, went (by accident) on 'red alert'. For six incredible minutes, the United States' 'red alert' signalled a nuclear war to begin at 3.40. Jet fighters took to the air. B-52 bombers were readied for take-off.

But it was all a ghastly mistake. The press reported next day: 'World War III could have begun in six minutes of madness' – meaning that the arms race had slipped into top gear. Apparently, 'they' did not know that their computer machine was connected to the early-warning system across the Western Defence Bases, which received a clear warning that the United States was *under attack*! It took six minutes before the North American Air Defence Command (NORAD) in Colorado realized that an error had been made when feeding in details of a phoney missile attack coming from over the North Pole. Margaret Thatcher was never told about it, it seems, because the mistake was discovered by the RAF before 'she needed to be informed'! Within 30 seconds they had received the reassuring answer: 'computer error'.

Who will answer 'computer error' next time, when a flight of wild geese across the North Pole sets all the bells ringing across this Heath-Robinson contraption that we have built in the name of 'security'? Questioned in the House of Commons two days later about why 'the Americans have the right [*sic*] to initiate the use of these weapons without consultation' (i.e. the new 572 'upgraded' warheads for NATO), the Defence Minister, Francis Pym, replied: 'This is not a dual key, it is a single key, but there are consultative processes, long established, which successive governments have thought to be adequate in all circumstances for the purpose.'

Unfortunately, that was not Mr Pym's last word. On 9 June 1980 he was again explaining away two further 'false computer warnings of a Soviet attack' happening within four days of each other. He assured the House that 'the computers are interlinked on both sides of the Atlantic', and that all this was 'entirely a defensive mechanism'. With a single key?

Nuclear bombs are unreliable servants. Under controlled situations, specialized bombs dropped on the ill-fated *Torrey Canyon* in 1968 failed to explode in the damaged ship, thus creating an additional hazard to the Channel shipping. In 1978 the accuracy of the bombing of another foundering oil-tanker depended on which way the winds were blowing.

Referring to the Soviet satellite which went astray in Canada in 1978, Frank Allaun MP drew attention to the accidental discharge of a nuclear-carrying missile. 'Sooner or later it is going to happen,' he said:

There are more than 10,000 of them poised for instant action East and West of the vertical frontier through the heart of Europe. The United States deploys over 30,000 nuclear warheads throughout the world. The Soviet Union also has a vast, though smaller, arsenal. Then there are the submarine-carried nuclear missiles on both sides. Electronic accidents have occurred, fortunately for us all without calamitous effects – so far. However, a crazy submarine commander could misinterpret or disobey a signal. And though there are electronic locks on some of the weapons, even electronic locks can be picked.

But the six minutes to zero did not happen in a vacuum. The Pentagon-planners and their Johnnies-come-lately in the Kremlin have been filling up the earth's vacuums with military hardware as fast as they can on the first-come-first-served principle. The Indian Ocean – proclaimed a zone of peace by Africans and Asians and most of the UN – is being festooned with nuclear bases from Somalia to Pakistan. Britain callously turned out the native islanders of Diego Garcia to make room for a new United States base, which is expanding fast now that the Russians are in Afghanistan. Somalia is actually switching over a former Soviet-occupied naval port to the Americans. United States warships and aircraft carriers went speeding to the Arabian Gulf, when Iran impounded the 53 US Embassy staff at Teheran.

It is in *this* starkly irrational context (not as featured in colourful scenarios of James Bond) that the fate of millions is being put at the mercy of military computer errors.

We know all too well today that when religious fanaticism compounds public fears with political arrogance, as it does across the Middle East, it can take only a handful of unstable bigots to imperil the common peace. Little wars are not local anymore. Today they are the spark-plugs for Armageddon. 'We are in a war situation,' proclaimed an enraged ayatollah: 'It is a

4

struggle between Islam and blasphemy.' Inevitably, the arms race has since produced an over-reaction that has reached the limits of the absurd.

On the other side of chaos, however, a statesman of wider vision and deeper acquaintance with Russian problems, George Kennan (former US Ambassador to Moscow), can tell his fellow citizens: 'In the official American interpretation of what occurred in Afghanistan, no serious account appears to have been taken of such specific factors as geographic proximity, ethnic affinity of peoples on both sides of the border, and political instability in what is, after all, a border country of the Soviet Union.'

During the last three decades, mankind has several times approached the brink of oblivion. But 'brinkmanship' did not start with Stalin. It became almost a way of life before that; Richard Nixon, who said: 'I have only to press that button . . .', idle threat though it may have been, took us pretty close to it more than once. How many more times can this happen, until the lemmings follow each other over the brink?

It has proved increasingly difficult, however, to set the perils of the present East-West confrontation against the permanent benefits of a new mutual security system through the UN, based on co-existence. Opponents of the World Disarmament Campaign glory in the have-you-stopped-beating-your-wife logic. Sir Gilbert Longden, for example, asks: 'What do you do when the rulers of the Soviet Union, upon whom public opinion has no effect, continue regardless to pile up arms and armaments far beyond those necessary for defence? Does the Campaign seek unilateral disarmament by Nato, or even by Great Britain alone; or does it not?' (*The Times*, 7 April 1980).

The fallacy and the absurdity of this kind of unilateral selectivity becomes obvious to the serious student who draws his facts and figures – as we shall do in the chapters that follow – from impartial sources such as SIPRI (the Swedish International Peace Research Institute) and the statistical services of the United Nations, who have no incentive to 'cook' their data to bolster up some forthcoming war budget against an outside enemy.

International efforts to 'control' the mad momentum of a hair-triggered arms race have so far produced no significant

5

results. They flounder on public ignorance and national egotism. On the contrary, the year 1980 ushered in a decade of cynicism, when – always on the pretext of some newly discovered 'Russian threat' to Europe – eleven members of NATO introduced 11,270 new weapons. Moreover, the governments of what is called the Eurogroup announced that their defence spending had risen by $20 billion in 1979; and they predicted that their contributions to world suicide would rise still higher in 1980. (They had already spent $50 billion on defence in 1978 and $70 billion in 1979.)

In the meantime, military technology advances as rapidly as human ingenuity and the stock market allows. Yesterday's science fiction becomes today's reality – and tomorrow's doom. It is no longer only a competition in quantity, but also quality; not numbers of weapons, but 'capacity' for indiscriminate destruction. This mad race has already become a war of technologies; of robots, not men. This is what was meant by 'updating' NATO's 'theatre' weapons in the 1980s (no James Bond scenario about *this* theatre!), meaning 572 super-super-warheads (each 20 times more terrible than Hiroshima). The Pentagon, *who holds the keys*, has decreed to Brussels that 160 of these should be planted on British soil.

Yet, if nuclear war came in Europe, our national societies would cease to exist. Nuclear deterrence is a nihilist doctrine, without morality, without reason, without hope. But it has become an article of Western faith; and the whole population of Europe – East and West – is trapped by it. Mutual assured destruction (MAD) has become the most morally indefensible strategy ever devised in the history of warfare. But, today it is the established policy of the big powers – a Satanic ideology legalized by treaties such as NATO. And the Russians, who are always behind the West, have followed suit. The Warsaw Pact was formed in 1955, after West Germany was brought into NATO (1949). There are plenty of battlefields on which to fight the good fight against the Soviet ideology and its contemptible totalitarian conception and mis-practice of human rights, but a nuclear battlefield is not one of them.

Exactly what human values, we ask, what national interests, are worth defending with weapons of genocidal destruction? Where are human rights, when millions of human beings are

6

reduced to mathematical coefficients on nuclear targets? We are so mentally paralysed by the false rhetoric of the arms race that the horror weapons we shall study in these chapters have to be given innocent-sounding names. And our whole 'defence' psychology today is being promoted by statesmen who do not know where they are going. We have become so inured to violence – impersonal, automated violence – that our moral judgment has become impaired by the apocalyptic calculations of a new breed of deterrence strategists, who are now asking: 'How many million deaths would be 'acceptable' in a nuclear war? How much megatonnage would be *needed* for national defence?' But no one answers, because there are no answers.

We have become the Age of Violence. When a Member of Parliament stands up in the same House of Commons debate mentioned above, and asserts: 'The decision of Brussels with the statement of President Carter on substantially increasing the American defence budget is the best news for peace and freedom since the Soviet Union deployed the SS-20 against us; I thank Mr Pym for his courage in giving leadership to the alliance' – are he and his supporters aware of the contribution they are making to the banked-up violence and moral degradation that is destroying our society?

This cancer of endemic military war runs through all lands and all social systems like a collective death wish. 'Whom the Gods would destroy, they first make mad' can be seen today on every level of national and international life. Dr Eric Martin, a Swiss, formerly President of the International Red Cross, says: 'For the last 20 years, violence in all its forms has been spreading over the planet in a frightening manner.' And he adds: 'Contrary to what might have been hoped or claimed, it is now evident that torture is not a remnant of a barbaric age, destined to disappear with the progress of civilization. Virtually eliminated from European States by the end of the nineteenth century, it has come back in full force, even within nations that claim to be in the forefront of social and legal progress.'

From the Third World, Judge Keba M'Baye, President of the Supreme Court of Senegal and President of the UN Human Rights Commission, has probed even deeper into our common sickness: 'The execrable crimes of the Second World War seem to have accustomed the human soul to the worst forms of

7

cruelty. It is as if the barbarity sleeping in every man has been liberated in some individuals. Those among them who hold a scrap of authority giving them the power to subdue or destroy their neighbour do not fail to use it.'

No one could have described the psychotic springs of the arms race in a shorter sentence. The psychotic personality may well have some genuine grounds in his original derangement: it is simply that he has lost touch with reality. Whatever its earlier moral motivation, that is what the arms race has become today. It has passed beyond moral or political control.

Not only big wars are the building blocks of violence. From an unexpected quarter, an Irishman of vision, Dr Desmond Moran, the coroner at the inquest into the deaths of Earl Mountbatten of Burma and three other members of his boating party in August 1979, urged politicians to make greater efforts to achieve peace in Ireland. At the end of the inquest, Dr Moran said: 'It is now unfortunately obvious to us all that outrages of this sort are one of the main problems society has to face in the latter half of the twentieth century.' And he added some simple but deeply moving words:

I believe it is necessary to stress again the great responsibility that parents and teachers of any nation have in the way they interpret history and pass it on to the youth of their country. I believe that if history could be taught in such a fashion that it would help to create harmony among people rather than division and hatred, it would serve this nation and all other nations better.

The worldwide campaign to stop the arms race and combat the violence that sustains it will be reflected in the positive proposals that find a central place in these pages. Yet at the outset we must admit that there can be found no panacea that can be compressed into a single rallying cry or presented in a neat political capsule. Wars can be won on national slogans, but peace can only be won on international understanding. And that is a hard discipline which cannot happen at once. There can be no higher form of patriotism than the kind of world loyalty for which this book pleads. That undoubtedly must start in our schools; but it must eventually run through the whole of life. It

8

is in the minds of men that the institutions of peace must be constructed. And the first step is to find out what are the facts – to define the disease that has corrupted our minds and imperils our society. No cure can be easy or swift. But the time to stop the arms race leading to the 'execrable crime' of a third world war is *NOW*. For we shall not pass this way again.

Geneva, Switzerland
July 1980   James Avery Joyce

I
The Meaning of Overkill

(1) What World War III would be like

A third world war would be the *final* phase of the present contest for world hegemony between the so-called capitalism of the USA and the alleged communism of the USSR, with everyone else dragged in. But neither system would survive it. For the arms race does not have a winner. The following pages try to explain why.

Nobody knows how many people would be left on earth. Estimates vary. But, if any at all, they wouldn't be very many or very healthy. In fact, 'overkill', as now being planned by NATO and WAPO (the rival North Atlantic Treaty and Warsaw Pact Organizations) will take care of everything – leaving, as the saying is, 'not a wrack behind'.

So why are politicians and opinion-makers in the West so keen on backing overkill? Why are some of them now proclaiming its inevitability? Lord Chalfont, like Richard Nixon, bluntly says that World War III 'has already *begun*'. Air-Marshal Sir Neil Cameron, visiting China recently, hinted as plainly: 'We both have an enemy at our door, whose capital is Moscow.' Mrs Thatcher, then leader of the British Conservative Party, when in Peking in 1977, urged the Chinese to increase their overkill capacity against the Soviet Union. She launched into an anti-Russian crusade in Brussels on 23 June 1978 with this advice:

The NATO Alliance will always be our best source of security. Indeed the United States, who will remain the foremost member of that Alliance, has taken the lead in increasing her own contribution to our joint defence . . . Unless we learn, as the Soviet Union has learnt, to look at the landscape as a whole, we shall be consistently out-manoeuvred.

The present book, in tracing the causes and consequences of the arms race, will have much to say about allowing the Russians to decide our defence programmes for us. This pragmatic approach is bound to upset a lot of people who take the arms race for granted. They *assume* that they can 'live' with the threatened holocaust. They call this 'security'. So the more the merrier. But an increasing number of people are paying £2,500 for shelters to protect them from the effects of a nuclear attack over Britain. So they can't be very convinced about what their Government is saying about 'security'.

Yet few overworked politicians can give much time or thought to what will really happen to Planet Earth if their national arms build-ups continue at the present rate. They are too wrapped up in saving their faces and keeping an eye on the next election. They are in office for five or six years, or less. So are presidents. But the arms profiteers and the Russians-are-coming military complex have their programmes already fixed, covering the whole of the 1980s and beyond. The Cabinet never has time to discuss the perils of the arms race in depth, least of all what can be done to *stop* it.

Mrs Thatcher was not quite a lone horse in encouraging this supplementary arms race, roping in China as a new untried ally. At the height of the Afghanistan crisis, the Carter administration, too, was revealed as seeking China's co-operation in boosting both China's and Pakistan's defences against Soviet military 'pressure'. Proposals for arms increases came from both governments, but on their own terms. US-Chinese efforts to strengthen Pakistan's defences were seen as a step towards closer 'security' collaboration between Washington and its inveterate enemy Peking! Washington even asserted that 'the Soviets have *forced* us and the Chinese to see the world in the same way'.

Hence, closer security ties with Peking had become a new-

	NATO	Warsaw Pact	People's Republic of China
Population	554,800,000	365,700,000	900,000,000
GNP	$3,367 billion	$1,240 billion	$309 billion
Military spending	$175 billion	$139 billion	$23-28 billion
Military manpower	4,900,000	4,850,000	4,300,000
Strategic nuclear weapons	9,400	4,500	200?
Tactical nuclear weapons	22,000?	15,000?	N.A.
Tanks	25,250+	59,000	9,000
Anti-tank missiles	200,000+	N.A.	N.A.
Other armoured vehicles	48,000+	62,000+	3,500
Heavy artillery	11,400+	22,600+	20,000
Combat aircraft	8,900+	10,400	5,900
Helicopters	12,300	4,550	350
Major surface warships	522	247	22
Attack submarines (all types)	211	239	66

Table 1   Military resources of NATO, Warsaw Pact and the People's Republic of China. (The US Defense Department estimates of Warsaw Pact manpower include 750,000 uniformed civilian personnel making the total Warsaw Pact manpower 5.6 million.)
Source: US Department of Defense

fangled way for the United States to respond to Moscow's actions in Afghanistan. In other words, the more unstable the situation, the more arms are poured into it. This piecemeal hit-and-miss management (or non-management) of the arms race has merely shifted the beginnings of World War III from central Europe or the Middle East to the Far East. Where next? But it doesn't give security to anyone, it doesn't give peace.

So what this book sets out to do first of all is 'to look at the landscape as a whole' and ask what World War III would be like if this suicidal helter-skelter death game is not halted in time. Its conclusions, as will be seen, are very different from those of the sophisticated hawks, British and American, who get all the media publicity but who contribute nothing to our sanity or safety. In this book we shall call the arms race not just a spade, but what Lt-General E. L. M. Burns of Canada has defined it as: *'megamurder'*. Megamurder means that we have now stored up three tons of TNT for every person on earth – all at the mercy of that *one key* in Washington.

Nothing in this book will seek to minimize the threat of nuclear war that hangs over us. Nothing in this book will lessen the need to prepare ourselves against it. Nothing in this book proposes a no-win policy or no-defence programme on the part of the British Government – or of any government. Nothing in this book will underestimate the peril facing the ordinary people if their government takes the wrong action or no action. Nothing in this book condones the military aggression in Afghanistan by a country that is constantly calling for a 'Treaty on the Non-Use of Force in International Relations'.

What this book does propose is action that is quite the reverse to our present posture of defence and defiance based upon theories and traditions that have had their day and can no longer work. What this book does advocate is an abandonment of alleged 'defence' measures which are determined by national decisions and based on military alliances which, by their nature, are bound to fail. What this book does do is to call for a fundamental revision of these attitudes and procedures so that, step by step, the present anarchy of states is replaced by a global order based on the principles of the UN Charter.

There is nothing illegal or unpatriotic about that. Members of the UN are committed to act in accordance with those specific procedures and to pursue universal and complete disarmament. It is precisely because we have reneged or side-stepped the UN that we are in the mess we are in. A deliberate decision to stop rearming and turn all the mental and material energies of the arms race into a world system of international co-operation through the UN is the moral duty of all citizens and a legal obligation of all governments. Not all citizens will see this as plainly as others, nor will all governments act as resolutely as others. But there can be no question that the Western nations, now dominated by the United States military hierarchy, must lead the other nations in establishing action programmes to implement their commitments to *stop* arming and work jointly and singly for a disarmed world.

This book should leave no doubt that by repudiating the national policies that make the arms race inevitable, the responsible citizen is fulfilling his most sacred responsibilities to his own country and to the world community. That this step demands a fundamental change of personal attitudes and national postures goes without saying. We have long passed the point where orthodox excuses or trivial goodwill gestures can accomplish great ends. It has been well said: 'For big ills, small remedies are no remedy at all.' And we are not proposing in this book small remedies to stop megamurder.

The reason why the senior Canadian General E. L. M. Burns calls all the subterfuges of a 'limited' nuclear war – even 'winning' a nuclear war – 'megamurder', is simply because, in a single short sentence: 'War has *become* megamurder.' Under the Hague Convention of 1907 the civilized nations agreed that the right of belligerents to adopt means of injuring the enemy 'was not unlimited'. The laws of war did not permit unarmed civilians to be killed deliberately.

However, in the fifty years that followed the Hague Convention, all that has been changed ... If the mass of nuclear weapons which now exists is used in war, it will mean the killing of millions of women, children and old men who bear no arms and who bear no responsibility for warlike decisions. Megaton bombs will cause mega-deaths. Is it wrong to call this not war, but mega-murder? (*Megamurder*, 1966)

14

When he left the Canadian service, Lt-General Burns joined the UN Truce Supervisory Service operating in Palestine between Jews and Arabs. He confesses that this assignment was the toughest in his career, i.e. keeping peace in a cauldron of fear and hatred and miscalculation. He says in his book *Megamurder*: 'The nightmare of the Western world and of the Soviet Union is that any day instantaneous death may come to millions upon millions of their populations, with the simultaneous destruction of the cities, the structures, the machines and the stored knowledge upon which civilizations depend.'

He is not alone in this belief. Herman Kahn, a conservative American scholar and leading research analyst on war, brought these fears into the open years ago in a way that shocked many people. In his 1959 book *On Thermonuclear War* he estimated with scientific detachment the results at that time of the destruction of 53 of the greatest metropolitan areas of the United States, as could well happen in so-called 'nuclear exchange' with the Soviet Union. The casualties which the American people would suffer might amount to 90,000,000. If, however, 70 per cent of the population of the 53 great metropolitan areas were *evacuated* – a vast undertaking requiring many months and many billions of dollars to build fall-out shelters in the less populated parts of the country – and *if* large stocks of everything needed to enable the survivors to live and rebuild the shattered country were laid by, then perhaps only 5,000,000 'would need' (*sic*) to die outright. This scenario seems over-optimistic in view of the much later data we shall deal with in this book. And Professor Kahn omitted to mention what sort of society would follow 'survival'. We shall refer later on to a British scholarly inventor of war games, General Sir John Hackett, who also fails to favour us with a picture of a *liveable* world, after all his own 'ifs' have come out to the satisfaction of mice and men, i.e. when the good guys have won a nuclear war against the Russians.

Lt-General E. L. M. Burns points out, however, that all these prophets of a nuclear war do not, and cannot, know what they are talking about. He says: 'There have been only two occasions, separated by a couple of days, when overkill weapons were used in actual warfare; hence it is necessary to imagine what will happen when the thousand-fold more powerful and more numerous thermonuclear weapons of today are used.' A distinguished soldier himself, he reminds us:

> As no general or admiral has any *real* experience of nuclear warfare, the pre-1945 theory of military tactics and strategy, built up from military history and criticism, provides little guidance. Thus the scientist, by his training, is probably as well able to determine how these new weapons systems should be used as is the military man.

Since the 1950s, however, scientists have been spending more energy publishing books warning us about the catastrophe to be expected than on devising practical policies to avoid it. So there exists a triple gap in public awareness – the active generals tell us it is all right, the scientists tell us it is not all right, and the politicians tell us nothing. In the United States, successive administrations, hoping somehow to reduce the danger which the mere existence of nuclear arms creates, have developed comforting theories about 'arms control'. Of course, it never works. But the basic idea is that nations having nuclear armaments should limit, by treaty or convention, their numbers and even their *use in war* – but without abolishing them. The word 'control' is never defined. It is preceded by adjectives like 'effective' or 'adequate'. Thus, the fantasy of 'arms control' has become the enemy of disarmament, which means something quite different from control.

The continuing fiasco at the SALT II proceedings revealed that 'arms control', conducted by men who distrust each other and who rigidly believe in mutual deterrence, rests on a fallacy and an illusion. That was why President Carter could only hope to get the Treaty (which he had negotiated face to face with Brezhnev) ratified by his own Senate by *raising* his arms budget by more than three per cent, even offering four and one half per cent; and also being compelled to agree to instal the most hideous and expensive killer of all, the MX – described later – as a sop to his hawks.

Only a handful of people, relative to this massive arms build-up, are standing up to be counted against such iniquities. Yet they include some of the most respected and intelligent leaders of our time. We shall cite their testimony in the course of this book. But public opinion is not altogether silent, in spite of the mass media smoke screen. This bi-polarization of nuclear destruction between the US and USSR is more and more seen to be a criminal conspiracy by two superpowers and their hangers-on, and completely irrelevant to the real pressing problems of our planet in the 1980s and beyond. The Brandt Commission, which reported in the spring of 1980, put this into perspective. They said:

We are increasingly confronted, whether we like it nor not, with more and more problems which affect mankind as a whole, so that solutions to these problems are inevitably internationalized. The globalization of dangers and challenges – war, chaos, self-destruction – calls for a domestic policy which goes much beyond parochial or even national items. We see signs of a new awareness that mankind is becoming a single community; but so far they have not been strong enough to stem the drift. In the short period since our Commission first met, in December 1977, the international situation has gone from bad to worse. It is no exaggeration to say that the future of the world can rarely have seemed so endangered.

The Third World and the non-aligned countries represent more people than are now being pitted against each other by their leaders in an unwinnable Armageddon. The North-South Dialogue, which aims to feed the world's 500 million hungry children and to reduce the poverty and misery of undeveloped peoples, is a more viable guarantee of peace and security than NATO's and WAPO's rival arsenals. The abomination of an East-West suicide pact overshadows a better life for the Earth's peoples with a mushroom cloud.

The hypocrisy of a NATO *versus* WAPO hara-kiri projected into the 1980s was brilliantly summed up by a speech to American scientists in Philadelphia on 8 November 1979, by Lord Zuckerman. The British Government's Chief Scientific Adviser from 1964 to 1971 stated that:

the so-called 'missile gap' turned out to have been a myth. [This was an earlier form of the 'Russian threat'.] Indeed, the

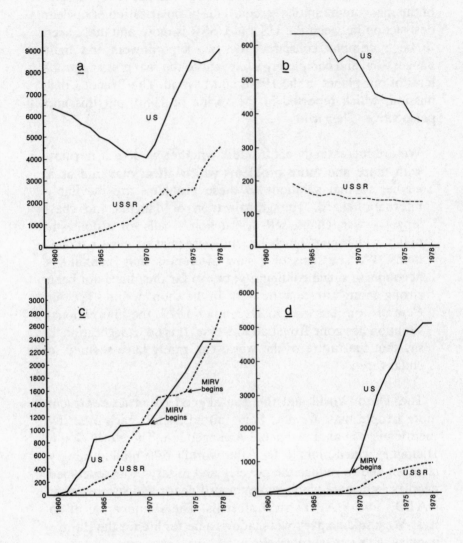

Fig. 1 (a) Total strategic nuclear weapons, United States and USSR; (b) number of long-range bombers, US and USSR; (c) nuclear weapons on land based missiles, US and USSR; (d) nuclear weapons on submarine missiles, US and USSR. These graphs cover *strategic* nuclear weapons; they do not include the even larger number of *tactical* nuclear weapons on both sides. The US has approximately 30,000 nuclear weapons, the Soviets approximately 20,000.
Source: US Center for Defense Information

Russians then started pressing hard to close the gap which *they* had perceived. This added another dimension to the arms race ... But even at the worst moments of the Cold War, neither side was prepared to risk hostilities which would result in what was euphemistically called 'a level of unacceptable damage'.

And what were his conclusions? Lord Zuckerman continued: 'The process of the nuclear race clearly has no logic. In the early 1970s, when Dr Henry Kissinger occupied high political office, he declared that no meaning could any longer be attached to the concept of nuclear superiority.' And he added:

More recently, at a meeting in Brussels last September, when talking about the 'modernization' of NATO's nuclear armoury, he [Kissinger] is reported as having said that the European allies of the United States should not keep asking the United States 'to multiply strategic assurances that we cannot possibly mean, or if we do mean, we should not want to execute, because if we execute we risk the destruction of civilization'.

And finally: 'No stronger endorsement than this could ever be sought for the paradox enunciated by York and Wiesner [physicists] in 1964 – that *the continued growth of nuclear arsenals does not increase, but decreases national security*.' (Our italics).

Yet, in the same columns of *The Times* where this speech appeared, we read that 'in the event of war, British troops on the European mainland would feel they were fighting for nothing if the people they were trying to defend were left totally unprotected'. Thus warned a Greater London Young Conservatives' booklet; so it suggested placing civil defence information in telephone directories, libraries and citizens' advice bureaux!

Nuclear weapons have not been used in war since August 1945. So all the hard-core facts about both their short-term and long-term effects relate to that horrendous month. There are varying estimates of the casualties at Hiroshima and Nagasaki. It has proved difficult to estimate the exact numbers of exposed people who may have died after *escaping* from the city. Official estimates are that only 78,000 were killed outright and 84,000 injured at Hiroshima, and 27,000 were killed and 41,000 injured at Nagasaki. But, in addition, there were thousands *missing* in both towns.

Some 45,000 of the fatal casualties at Hiroshima died on the day of the explosion, and some 20,000 during the following four months, as a result of traumatic wounds, burns and radiation effects. There are no estimates of the numbers who may have died from the effects of induced radioactivity experienced during rescue work in the city. Most of the medical facilities in Hiroshima were in the devastated area. Next to immediate medical problems, the most serious challenge to those who survived the direct effects of the explosion were problems of water supply, housing and food. To those who did not suffer immediately these difficulties compounded the profound psychological effects of the disaster. Twenty years after the bombings there was still an excessive sensitivity to the thought of radiation hazard. As late as September 1978 a 75-year-old Hiroshima atomic bomb survivor despondent over her lingering illness caused by exposure to radiation jumped to her death from the fifth floor of a nursing home in Tokyo where she was being treated for radiation-related lumbago, while a day later another survivor committed suicide because of radiation poisoning.*

Apart from the effects which ionizing radiation had on the victims of the explosions, the survivors were also exposed to the hazards of radiation both in terms of latent diseases occurring in the individual (somatic effects) and of changes in hereditary material (genetic effects). Exposure to repeated moderate doses of nuclear radiation is conducive to leukaemia – a disease which is associated with a malignant over-production of white blood cells. The incidence of leukaemia in the survivors of Hiroshima and Nagasaki was observed to be increasing in 1948 and reached a peak in 1952. It still remains much higher than in the population of the rest of Japan. While the incidence of the disease increased in all age groups, it did so more sharply in young people.†

Since every city has its own individuality, communications

*UPI report, 3 and 4 September 1978
†UN Publication, A/6858

20

and food supplies, a realistic picture of what *would* happen cannot be derived unless one considers a real city. One such study was made in 1968 by UN specialists of a city with a population of just over one million people. It was assumed that a one-megaton nuclear weapon had burst at ground level. Using the experience of Hiroshima and Nagasaki, and estimating on the basis of the results of carefully designed weapons experiments, the following figures of casualties emerged:

Killed by blast and fire	270,000
Killed by radioactive fall-out	90,000
Injured (of whom 15,000 were in the area of fall-out and thus exposed to the effects of radiation)	90,000
Uninjured (of whom 115,000 were in the area of fall-out)	710,000

This report to the UN in 1968 was presented by a group of consultant experts, whose members were: Wilhelm Billig, Chairman of the State Council for Peaceful Uses of Atomic Energy, Poland; Alfonso Léon de Garay, Director of the Genetics and Radiobiology Programme, National Nuclear Energy Commission, Mexico; Vasily S. Emelyanov, Chairman of the Commission on the Scientific Problems of Disarmament of the Academy of Sciences of the Union of Soviet Socialist Republics; Martin Fehrm, Director General of the Research Institute of Swedish National Defence; Bertrand Goldschmidt, Director of External Relations and Planning, Atomic Energy Commission, France; W. Bennett Lewis, Senior Vice-President, Science, Atomic Energy of Canada Limited; Takashi Mukaibo, Professor, Faculty of Engineering, University of Tokyo, Japan; H. M. A. Onitiri, Director, Nigerian Institute of Social and Economic Research, University of Ibadan, Nigeria; John G. Palfrey, Professor of Law, Columbia University, New York, USA; Gunnar Randers, Managing Director, Norwegian Institute for Atomic Energy; Vikram A. Sarabhai, Chairman, Atomic Energy Commission of India; Sir Solly Zuckerman, Chief Scientific Adviser to Her Majesty's Government, United Kingdom. This is what they also said:

The enormity of the shadow which is cast over mankind by

21

the possibility of nuclear war makes it essential that its effects be clearly and widely understood. It is not enough to know that nuclear weapons add a completely new dimension to man's powers of destruction. Published estimates of the effects of nuclear weapons range all the way from the concept of the total destruction of humanity to the belief that a nuclear war would differ from a conventional conflict, not in kind, but only in scale. The situation, however, is not as arbitrary as opposing generalizations such as these might suggest. There is one inescapable and basic fact. It is that the nuclear armouries which are in being already contain large megaton weapons every one of which has a destructive power greater than that of all the conventional explosive that has ever been used in warfare since the day gunpowder was discovered. Were such weapons ever to be used in numbers, hundreds of millions of people might be killed, and civilization as we know it, as well as organized community life, would inevitably come to an end in the countries involved.

Continuing this report, approximately one-third of all the inhabitants would thus have been killed as a result of blast and fire or from a radiation dose received in the first two days. Practically all the inhabitants of the central area of the city, an area of about five by six kilometres, would have been killed. Any not immediately killed in the central area would have died from nuclear radiation. Most of the 90,000 of the city's population who would have suffered non-lethal injuries would have been serious casualties. Rescue operations would have been greatly impeded by radioactive fall-out.

Those, fortunately there are only a few, who talk glibly about 'winning' a nuclear war have not looked at what the geneticists are saying about the changes that ionizing radiation induces in plants, animals, and human beings. What kind of survival they propose to 'win' at the end of it is discreetly ignored. The aforementioned UN report is modest, but it concludes:

In general, the long-term genetic effects of nuclear radiation in living organisms are cumulative. While no visible injury would accompany the induction of genetic changes in the exposed individuals, undesirable consequences would arise in

22

succeeding generations. It is reasonably certain that a population which had been irradiated at an intensity sufficient to kill even a few per cent of its members, would suffer important long-term consequences. (UN report)

Countless dead bodies and seriously wounded people, who barely breathed, were left on the road or the river-banks of the city. Medical supplies were used up immediately because of the unimaginable number of wounded. The untreated people took their last breath moaning, 'Give me water.' What is now called radiation sickness soon appeared. People began suffering from diarrhoea as if they had dysentery, losing clumps of their hair, and developing purple coloured spots on their skin which made them look like a map. Such people soon died, their bodies full of big maggots they were too weak to remove. (Eyewitness at Hiroshima, 1945)

The word 'defence', however, has recently taken on a meaning appropriate to the Stone Age – or at least the battle of Waterloo. The British Government's civil defence plans are to

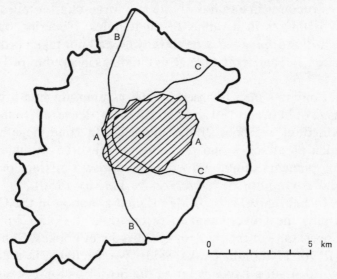

Fig.2 Distribution of casualties following a nuclear attack. A is a line enclosing central area of 6×5 km. where practically the whole population would be killed. B is a line through a point 2.5 km. west of bomb-burst, marking limit of fall-out. C marks the area inside which a person would receive a lethal dose from fall-out in 48 hours if he stayed in the open. *Source*: UN Report, 1968

23

be given greater priority now that SS-20 Russian missiles will carry pre-targeted warheads, and the supersonic Backfire bomber is to be added, 'counter-poised' to Britain's agreed installation of 160 'upgraded' American-built and manned ground-launched Cruise missiles. Hence the Government is likewise thinking of 'upgrading' civil defence.

Britain's Home Defence Gamble is an interesting local document, published by the Conservative Political Centre. It states: 'Since 1968, when home defence was last drastically cut back, successive governments have gambled that there will be enough time when international crises occur, to enable an effective policy for the home defence of the country to be re-established. If the gamble fails, millions of people will die unnecessarily.' [*sic*]

But has it not occurred to any government since 1968 that 'defence' can no longer be so 'civil'? As the document clearly shows:

One megaton is the equivalent of one million tons of TNT. The effect of a single one-megaton air-burst over County Hall, London, would be the complete destruction of brick structures in a radius of one and three-quarter miles, ignition of fabrics in a radius of eight miles; blistering burns in a *radius of nine miles* on those who had not taken proper shelter [*sic*] and light damage to buildings in a radius of 11 miles.

London's plan is based on the assumption that a megatonnage of between 180 and 200 could be 'delivered' to the United Kingdom by about 200 weapons, in the one-megaton range. Such an attack would probably be delivered within 24 hours, the planners think, and would comprise a mixture of both air and ground bursts. (*Observer*, 16 January 1980).

In February 1980 70 MPs signed a motion in the Commons urging the Government to reconstitute the old Civil Defence Corps. One of the signatories, Miss Janet Fookes, Conservative MP for Plymouth, Drake, said: 'We are living in a dangerous world. I am a hawk as far as the Soviet Union is concerned. I don't trust their Government at all.' (*The Times*, 8 February 1980). So we now know what the hawks are thinking. We can trust our shelters, but we can't trust the Russians.

Perhaps the most apposite commentary on this renewed 'civil

defence' debate in the 1980s was also the shortest. It appeared from a correspondent (Mr B. J. Greenwood) in *The Times* in these terms:

> Sir, I must thank you for your fascinating series of articles on Civil Defence. It is indeed a great comfort to learn that, when the holocaust arrives, our Government will be safely housed in a three-storey bunker deep under a wooded hill in the country. What a shame that they will no longer have a population to govern!

But can anyone of any political party in Britain recall what has been Britain's contribution to *disarmament* and peace during this decade of grace? Has any government spokesman been honest enough to admit that (on the foregoing facts) *there is no such thing as civil defence*? Has anybody during twelve years of discussion on measures for universal and complete disarmament heard the ringing tones of British delegates announcing *British* disarmament plans or, at any time, accepting and approving the many Soviet and Eastern European and Third World proposals, tabled again and again at the UN? Where has Britain stood on these crucial debates for banning of nuclear weapons? Will Britain's acceptance of 160 of NATO's new 572 megamurder weapons in Europe compensate for a shameful decade of neglect and silence? Cannot they yet see and say that the only form of 'civil defence' in the 1980s *is to stop the arms race*?

'Britain's vulnerability', says Councillor Ronald Huzzard,

> arises from our so-called defence policy which causes nuclear weapons targeted on other countries to be stationed in these islands. There is no conceivable protection against nuclear weapons, whether they are of the size which obliterated Hiroshima or the larger type now stockpiled by the two super-Powers. The 1978 United Nations special session stressed that the only security today lies through disarmament. (*Observer*, 2 April 1980).

Why the silent back-room scientists are no match for the strident militarists is because 50 per cent of them are now working for the military-industrial complex itself. The military man, it is true, whether soldier, sailor or airman, still thinks of himself as the defender of his country. He assumes that in carrying out this duty, there should be no limits to the degree of force which he can employ when under the authority of his government.

But if we ask the simple question: 'What, in any country, *is* the principal requirement of the military?', the answer is, bluntly, '*an enemy*'. Since World War II, the United States has never lacked an enemy. The expansion in Eastern Europe of communist political control, under the aegis of a victorious Soviet army as long ago as 1944, produced the initial psychological threat. But, today, a million Americans, including their families, are stationed in West Germany – 35 years after World War II *ended*. So is BAOR – a throw-back to World War I. As mutual fears intensified, they focused on the possibility of nuclear war, to stop an implacable enemy at the gates. Yet the mythical syndrome of an undefined 'world communist conspiracy' that dominated American thinking, was exploded when China was discovered to be the *real* enemy of Russia. But it had, meanwhile, bolstered up the armaments budgets of the United States and its allies. The bolstering still goes ahead, while China and Russia now exchange insults and threats with each other, while the West looks on helplessly.

As time went on 'the enemy' became more and more *essential* to keep the defence system on its toes. The fear, threat or some other menace of 'the enemy' has always had to be manufactured, even where it does not exist. Every Western arms budget increase is served up with Russian caviar to make it palatable. The Pentagon spends millions of dollars in propaganda on inflating this enemy. The press, with its selective news coverage, has kept the ball rolling. As a result, the Russians – negatively, it is true – have become an essential part of the Western way of life. (Or death?) Is it not ironical that the Soviet Union should have produced America's greatest modern industry – the war industry, an industry that grows, financially and even geographically, all the time?

A US Air Force study reported in 1978 that the proposed new MX missile system for the 1980s will cost between $20 and $27 billion and need an area of between 4,000 and 6,500 square miles – about the size of Connecticut. 'Full-scale engineering development is expected, however, to result in only 44,000 new jobs nationwide for workers in aerospace and related industries,' according to an Air Force statement on the proposed IBM and its mobile launching system. As the Rev. William Sloan Coffin, a leading US heretic has said: 'The arms race provides more and more jobs for machines and fewer jobs for people.'

How does this war-preparedness obsession work out on the official level? 'NATO's strategy of flexible response', says the US State Department's Bureau of Public Affairs (November 1979),

> is designed to enable the alliance *to respond to any level of initial action* by an aggressor, from demonstrations of force to full-scale hostilities. Our ability *to meet any threat* must pose a clear risk of unacceptable costs *to our potential enemies* – this is the crucial element needed to deter an aggressor from any level of initial action. This strategy requires a force structure – conventional, theatre nuclear, and strategic – which plainly shows that we have many options to influence the course of conflict. The logic of deterrence remains compelling; for 30 years it has helped preserve peace in Europe. [Our italics].

So what is Washington's conclusion? More and more and more: in other words: 'The alliance must modernize in order not to encourage Soviet misperceptions about our capabilities.' We notice how well the options worked over Iran and Afghanistan.

Whatever may still be Russian 'misperceptions', after all this time, the biggest sleight-of-hand in this fragile house of cards is that it has kept peace in Europe for 30 years. This is what has always been said about past arms races. That is what the man who fell from the 50th floor window muttered as he passed the 30th floor. But there is nothing sacrosanct about 30 years. Generals who talk like this are mesmerized by the short span of 20 years between World War I and World War II. Such comparisons are fallacious. They ignore the fact that there was no major European war between 1814 and 1914.

What the arms race has actually done to Europe can be seen

27

on three separate levels. First, it has split the continent into two insecure armed camps and has therefore diminished, not increased, the peace of Europe. Secondly, it has fed fear and hate into the minds of a whole new generation, who had no responsibility for the errors that led to World War II. Thirdly, its horror weapons and moral iniquity have spilled over into a hundred Third World nations outside Europe, so that Korea and China and Iran and Afghanistan, and a dozen African states, have all become the cat's-paws of both sides of a broken Europe; and the race is now reaching into the Indian Ocean.

We have demonstrated in this book how the concoction of coloured lie-words, beginning with Dulles' 'massive retaliation' and passing through 'phased responses' and 'deterrence' to the latest abomination called 'nuclear capability', has been so built into the false rhetoric of political debate and the columnists' jargon, that few people realize the intellectual degradation and spiritual corrosiveness of the brain-washing process to which they have been subjected these 30 years. For these reasons, the World Disarmament Campaign that is now gaining force around and through the UN – of which this book is a small harbinger – has to fight a Herculean battle over a terrain poisoned with ancient untruth and encumbered with the vestiges of man's savage ancestry.

The founders and joint-chairmen of this campaign are British. Lords Philip Noel-Baker and Fenner Brockway can be under no illusion as to the immensity of the revolutionary task to which they and their supporters have set their hand. We shall return to their endeavours later in this book; but, by placing their world campaign within the framework of the United Nations programmes and structures, to which over 150 governments are already legally committed, the organizers have confidently spelled out their policy as being directed:

> to achieve, by appropriate stages, the general and complete disarmament of all nations under strict and effective international control, together with the re-allocation of the resources so released to world development, that is to say, to the ending of world poverty and for the promotion of social justice and human welfare in all countries, developed and developing. (*The Times*, 2 April 1980).

28

(2) Line-up of the nukes

As the nuclear age has 'unfolded' (according to a State Department brochure) the United States and the Soviet Union have procured new kinds of strategic systems to deliver nuclear weapons. First these systems were bombers. Then the bombers were supplemented by land-based intercontinental ballistic missiles (ICBMs) and submarine-launched ballistic missiles (SLBMs). In the 1970s both nations increased their nuclear capabilities by deploying MIRVed missiles – missiles with several warheads that can be independently targeted. Today, the US and the USSR both have vast arrays of sophisticated nuclear weapons aimed at targets in each other's territory.

Both nations view the SLBMs as vital to their defence because, for the foreseeable future, they are virtually invulnerable to detection and attack.

Although the Soviets have about 950 SLBMs in 62 submarines [says the State Department], compared to our 656 in 41 submarines, MIRVing now enables us to deliver many more warheads than the Soviets can *from beneath the sea*. Also, our SLBMs are more accurate and most have greater throw-weight. Our submarines are quieter and harder to track, and we keep more of them on patrol at sea than do the Soviets. [Our italics].

The Soviet Navy is completing work on a new submarine described by Defense Department officials as the largest undersea vessel ever built. The huge vessel was spotted by US surveillance satellites when it was moved out of a construction shed at the naval yard on the White Sea. Based on the satellite photographs, intelligence analysts concluded that the submarine is about 480 feet long and 57 feet in diameter, making it larger in volume than the US Navy's new class of nuclear-powered Trident submarines. (*New York Times*, 8 May 1980).

Great Britain has, of course, been caught in this underwater net of terror weapons, and is locked there until the late 1990s. A decision has been made at the Ministry of Defence that Britain's 'independent' (*sic*) nuclear deterrent should be replaced

29

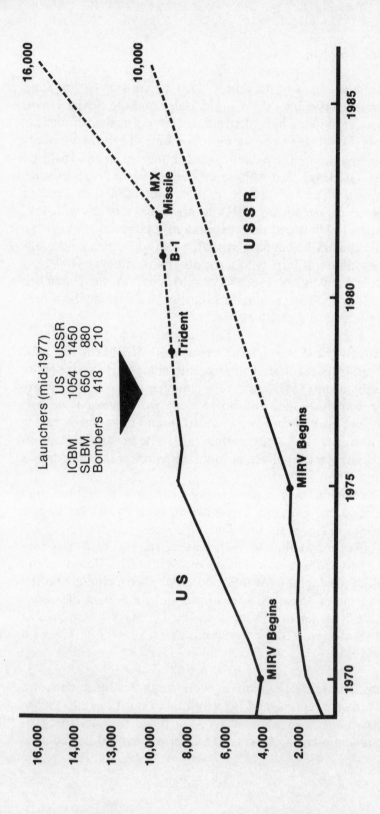

Fig.3 Nuclear warheads and launchers possessed and projected by US and USSR.

Source: US Department of Defense

in the 1990s by a fleet of five submarines carrying American Trident missiles fitted with British warheads. This Trident proposed purchase is a direct successor to the older Polaris missile. The plan is to have the first of the new submarines in service by the mid-1990s, with a fleet of five boats eventually replacing the Royal Navy's four Polaris submarines, so as to have at least two boats on patrol at any time. (*The Times*, 1 November 1979).

Each of them will probably carry 16 Trident I missiles, which are three-stage ballistic rockets with a range of 7,000 kilometres, currently under development for the US Navy. The Aldermaston Atomic Weapons Research Establishment may be asked to develop a new warhead carrying MIRVs, on which design work has already been done.

But the cost to Britain can hardly be less than £5,000 millions, if a Cabinet decision is made to go ahead with this monstrosity. However, the RAF are known to have some reservations about spending ten per cent of the defence budget on a so-called deterrent force during the peak four or five years of its development. One hope remains. The submarines will not be under construction until the early 1990s. *In 1982 the UN meets to seek a World Disarmament Convention and public campaigns in support of it have begun in earnest.*

Reverting to the two main adversaries, a third part of each country's strategic force is still intercontinental bombers. The US last year (1979) had 420 operational aircraft – more than twice as many as the USSR – and they carry heavier armament, more advanced electronics, and greater payloads. Although the Soviet Union has emphasized air defence, the US believes that it can count on most of its bombers to penetrate their defences.

The mutually induced threats the two countries face are nevertheless somewhat different. For example, China, France and the United Kingdom, although not parties to the SALT talks, have nuclear weapons of their own. Chinese missiles are at present too limited in range to pose a threat to the US, but not to the USSR.

Given these differences, it is difficult to compare the nuclear forces of the two sides and decide whether one has an overall advantage. The United States leads in deliverable warheads, the Soviets in vehicles to deliver them; the United States leads in bomber payload, and (assumed) submarine quality; but the Soviet Union leads in missile throw-weight, and is developing more new systems. Since both sides have gone to great lengths to ensure the survival of their retaliatory forces, the balance between them is now alleged to be in 'strategic equilibrium'. This means that neither side should be *tempted* to gain an advantage by trying to destroy the other's forces. But – and this is a big *BUT* – the arms race goes on, because each side tries to upset this balance in its own favour. The folly of this paper game was exposed recently by rumours that the US civilian intelligence agencies were quarrelling behind the scenes with the military about what that 'balance' was. The military contends that the job of comparing US and Soviet forces in an atomic struggle is the prerogative of the Joint Chiefs of Staff and the Defense Department rather than the CIA. Other paper strategists have remarked that the total missilry is so vast that a few megatons one side or the other no longer matters.

An agreed overall limit of 2,400 ICBMs, SLBMs, heavy bombers, and air-to-surface ballistic missiles for each side was agreed at Vladivostok at the 1974 summit meeting between President Ford and (then) General Secretary Brezhnev. Within these agreed limits, each side would be free to choose whatever 'mix' of forces it preferred. But two key issues – concerning the Soviet bomber known to us as Backfire and US Cruise missiles – were not settled. Disagreement on whether, or how, these weapons should be limited has played a large part in delaying a SALT II accord.

Last winter, however, the world lurched nearer to war. On 6 October 1979 President Brezhnev announced an immediate and unilateral, though limited, withdrawal of 1,000 tanks and 20,000 Russian troops from East Germany. He also offered a reduction in the number of SS-20 medium-range missiles if NATO did not proceed with the Cruise and Pershing II missiles. But this opportunity was shuffled off. Then came Afghanistan. When an offer to negotiate comes, the sensible thing is to seize it quickly and put it to the test. Instead, NATO chiefs decided to manufacture and deploy the 572 new nuclear missiles.

According to Rear-Admiral Gene R. La Rocque, director of the Washington Center for Defense Information, the traditional role of the military in all countries, in case of war, is to win:

The military profession, to be blunt, has always sought superiority. Military men tend to be uncomfortable with notions of military balance or equilibrium ... We feel reassured by big military establishments, we believe the security of our people is enhanced by spending for additional war-fighting and war-winning capabilities.

Addressing the UN Special Session on Disarmament on 13 June 1978, the Admiral stated that the United States had added more nuclear weapons to its arsenal than the Soviet Union, increasing from 4,000 strategic weapons in 1970 to 9,000 in 1978. During the same period the Soviet Union increased from 1,800 to 4,500 nuclear weapons. 'The US has maintained a two-to-one edge in deliverable nuclear weapons throughout the period 1970–78', he stated, and added: 'My experience in the United States military has convinced me that nuclear weapons have changed the traditional rules of warfare. To use an American phrase, "it's a whole new ball game".'

That Rear-Admiral La Rocque does not under-estimate the massive threat hanging over us was made clear in his address

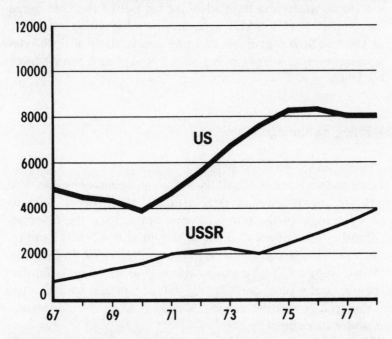

Fig.4   US and USSR operational strategic offensive warheads/bombs, 1967–77.
Source: US Center for Defense Information

33

when he stated that a recent top-level US Government study concludes that at a minimum 140 million people in the US and 113 million in the USSR would be killed in a major nuclear war. He concluded:'Almost three-quarters of their economies would be destroyed. In such a conflict, neither side could conceivably be described as a winner.' Nor would those in the rest of the world be safe. Radiation would poison vast stretches of the planet not directly involved in the war. And the threat of ozone damage and ecological disruption leaves us no assurance that the earth would remain habitable for life as we know it:

A desirable SALT agreement should slow the introduction of new weapons, reduce incentives and capabilities for starting a nuclear war, contain reasonable incentives to insure compliance by both sides and be explicitly clear and not leave ambiguities open to unilateral interpretation.

American and Soviet confidence in the arms control process needs to be reinforced if the danger of nuclear war is to be reduced. An agreement that reduces Vladivostok ceilings by ten per cent and imposes some qualitative limits on new weapons, while less than ideal, is far better than no agreement at all. Such a SALT agreement could reduce the growth of US and Soviet arsenals and prevent as many as 7,000 new nuclear weapons from being *added* to US and Soviet forces by 1985.

(3) Piling on the agony

So where do we go from here?

Later in this book we shall try to find some *new* answers. But, for the moment, we must deal with the old answers. Such as: follow the logic of the bomb, go one better than the Russians, or, simply, *more overkill*! That is just what the NATO summit conference decided in Brussels in November 1979. In fact, they said two things: (1) 'We must raise our arms budgets another three per cent a year' and (2) 'We will accept and spread across Europe 572 new super-nuclear weapons from the Pentagon – *and under its control*.'

These old answers amount to nothing less than 'piling on the agony'. They have added nothing to anyone's security. They involve a constant search for new 'generations' of weapons. Advances in technology are all the time ushering in a new spurt in the arms race. The race for quantity has become a race for quality; and nuclear war becomes more 'thinkable'. Included in the current US Defence Budget are proposed funds for:

(1) *The MX*, a mobile, land-based missile, and other 'improvements' in the US Minuteman III.
(2) *The Trident*, a huge submarine armed with 192 nuclear warheads.
(3) *The Cruise Missile*, a low-flying nuclear weapon aimed to land within 100 feet of the target, after a flight of 8,000 miles.

If some warheads are to be smaller in size, more of them can be carried together in a large MIRV and then fired independently at different targets. With more warheads available and more accurate means of directing them at targets, military planners can programme weapons to strike targets ranging from military installations and fortified missile silos to economic and industrial targets such as bridges, dams, power plants, and major storage areas. Anyone living close to these targets would be back in Hiroshima.

It is significant of the escape from reality of some governments in facing these qualitative changes in megamurder weapons that, according to Peter Hennessy, 'the Prime Minister has instructed her ministers to imitate her example and take a direct part in exercises designed to test plans for the transition to a conventional or a nuclear war'. And Mr Hennessy goes on to add:

One of the more intriguing chapters in *The War Book*, Whitehall's highly secret and immensely detailed contingency plan, was promulgated in the early 1950s, when stock was first taken of the Soviet Union's capacity to launch an atomic strike against the British Isles.

It deals with the role of the Chief Press Secretary to the Prime Minister in the transition period to nuclear war. He will be expected, according to *The War Book*, to take control of national newspapers and television. (*The Times*, 26 February 1980).

Whether the authors of this secret war games compilation are to be taken seriously or not, it is to be noted that *The Times* correspondent concludes his astonishing revelations by pointing out that:

the great weakness of the plan, according to an ultra-realistic official, is its touching expectation that anybody will be left in London to process the copy. 'Can you imagine,' he asked, 'all your compositors and all the broadcasting technicians happily catching their usual trains to work in the knowledge that a bomb might be dropped on London at any moment?'

World War III comes much closer because the temptation to strike such targets with these new weapons may persuade military planners to envisage 'limited' attacks, intended to fall short of an all-out thermonuclear war. (We shall take up this grievous miscalculation when we examine General Hackett's recent book on World War III.) This is a highly dangerous speculation since, apart from the appalling destructiveness of any 'limited' nuclear explosion, the other side would be most likely to respond with a counter-attack. So the whole situation would soon get out of control.

Since the neutron bomb can, for the moment, be dubiously classified as a 'conventional' weapon, we might look briefly at the other three nukes listed above. MX (or 'missile Experimental') is to be a land-based intercontinental ballistic missile (ICBM) designed to augment the existing force of Minuteman III. Besides being mobile, each MX would carry ten to 14 independently targeted warheads, each warhead possessing twice the explosive power and three times the accuracy of the Minuteman III. But its extra-special feature lies in an exotic subway system carved in the colourful deserts of the American south west, consisting of 300 covered trenches, each six to 25 miles long. This devil's subway is designed for *fighting a nuclear war*. Giant railway cars bearing intercontinental ballistic missiles will travel up and down the tunnels *so that the enemy won't know where they are*! Each missile can break through the earth and aim at enemy targets.

36

It is obvious that the MX is an extremely expensive system. Each missile is expected to cost $100 million, while the total costs for the system are estimated between $30 and $50 billion, if housed in 4,500 miles of tunnels, costing about $5 million a mile. The SALT II negotiations were held up because the US proposal for hiding land-based missiles among a cluster of empty, underground silos appeared to be incompatible with the terms of a new treaty *limiting* strategic arms until 1985. It met with great resistance from Moscow. (How can you 'limit' missiles that are not there?)

Under the US 'multiple aim point' idea, hundreds of missiles would be moved around thousands of empty launching silos in random fashion. The basic purpose of this 'shell-game' would be to complicate any effort by the Soviet Union to destroy US land-based missiles in a first-strike rocket attack. (The Russians are always assumed to strike first.)

And what effect will this infantile game of hide-and-seek have upon the Russians? Its threat could plainly cause the Soviet Union to hasten its development of qualitative nuclear weapon improvements. But, as a vastly richer country, which, unlike the Soviet Union, gained considerable financial and commercial benefits as a result of the last war, the United States can pursue – and is pursuing – a beggar-my-neighbour policy against the Soviet Union, whose struggling economy has long been a figure of fun for American cold warriors and cartoonists.

Studies of the Soviet economy reveal that Moscow has been able to meet each new threat from the Pentagon only by heavy economic and social sacrifices. Nowadays almost half the machinery produced in the Soviet Union is military equipment of some sort. This represents an alarming diversion of resources from investment badly needed to modernize Soviet industry. The Soviet Union has already paid a high price to catch up militarily with the West. But it will have to pay an even higher price to hang on to that position if military competition continues at this rate.

Investment to maintain equality with America in such a new round of weapons competition in the 1980s would have to be taken from diminishing funds, for the Soviet Union is well behind America in such new technological development, as, for example, 'miniaturization'. What will happen to the Soviet economy over the next ten years is that it will grow at a slower pace. During the 1980s this could be between three and three and a half per cent a year, which, as it happens, would be the same as is expected for the industrialized West. In other words, it will be Soviet citizens who will be the victims of the American build-up of these new weapons of mass destruction. But perhaps that is all part of the game?

The depressing world economic outlook for the next two years 1980–81, however, throws a deepening shadow over all the industrialized West. In Britain, for example, Treasury economists have warned the Chancellor that output in Britain may fall by as much as three and one half per cent in 1980, with a further drop in 1981. In one of the most depressing pre-Budget economic assessments ever made, they have also given a warning that the Government faces a deficit in 1981 of £9,500 million. The forecast for the drop in output foresees such a severe recession over the year ahead that it started a new round of soul-searching within the Treasury in March 1980 about the forecasting techniques used to predict the future. While, in the United States, the 'new' President, elected in November 1980, faces an economic challenge far more urgent and realistic than the perennial 'Russian threat'.

The scientific ingenuity and the mammoth expenditure involved in the gross insult to civilization which we have just described, and to which President Carter has *had* to give the OK, would have provided clinics, schools and shelter for the earth's 500 million sick and needy children. The Russians are already proposing to match it, of course, if the US goes ahead. But will that 'threat' prevent a total territory the size of Connecticut from being churned up to make the world's biggest nuclear arsenal?

There is another forgotten aspect of this digging of future graveyards for our children. The current world population is about 4,000 million. Yet, if present population trends continue there will be double that number – 8,000 million people – on earth *in only 35 years' time*. Our present diminishing land and food resources could not support them. This is because for many years thoughtless people and blind statesmen all over the

38

world have been plundering and polluting the earth's natural resources on land, in the air, on the rivers, and in and under the sea at such a rate as to pose a serious threat to the environment, which supports all forms of life. While the UN Environment Programme (UNEP) is starved of funds, equipment, and personnel, the military pollutionists are now driving up inflation in the US by turning needed land into a vast cemetery.

And yet another aspect: pollution of the atmosphere and the reduction of the vital protective ozone layer around the earth present two other perils. Scientists warn that, if continued unchecked, these trends could so vitiate our biosphere that ultimately its capacity to support life might be destroyed. What happens to mankind when MX missiles and the rest have eliminated the ozone layer protecting all life on earth?

The Trident is no mere sea-urchin! It is a nuclear-powered submarine over two football fields in length and five storeys high, more than twice the size of the Polaris and Poseidon submarines. It will carry as many as 24 nuclear missiles, each equipped with 17 independently targetable warheads. It is designed to wreak thermonuclear havoc on 408 separate targets by hurling 75–100 kilotons of explosive power at each one with nearly pinpoint (90 foot) accuracy. The US Navy plans 30 of these monstrosities to act for the rest of the century as the sea-leg of the strategic triad, ensuring American nuclear superiority over the USSR and providing an integral component in a potential first strike nuclear capability.

Britain is being pressured to buy five of them, plus the 160 land-based killers under the 1979 NATO-Pentagon compact in Brussels. There are, however, rumours of disagreement in the Cabinet and growing hostility from the Army as well as the RAF. The penny is now beginning to drop, in more senses than one. Given Britain's economic predicament, are we going to be able to afford Trident without huge cut-backs in equipment to the other two services?

The relative invulnerability of submarines makes them an important part of the US 'defensive' arsenal, since submarines could survive a nuclear attack – in theory – and would be able to retaliate. So the Pentagon tells us. The existing Polaris and Poseidon submarines were *already* capable of obliterating scores of cities with their multiple warheads. The main difference between them and Trident lies in the greater number, power, and accuracy of its missiles. And the Trident missile will double the Poseidon's 2,000-mile range. But it won't stop even there – unless we stop the arms race.

And the effect on the USSR? We have already noted that they are going one better. Trident will clearly be perceived by the Russians as transforming US submarines from (so-called) retaliatory weapons into *offensive* weapons, with 'silo-busting' potential. Submarines don't fight submarines, any more than tanks normally fight tanks; so the 'balance' doctrine does not apply as far as figures are concerned.

Each of them will cost over 1.7 billion dollars. Total programme costs are expected to exceed $30 billion. Some $8.8 billion has been spent to date, and the US programme is already a year behind schedule, as well as 50 per cent over its original budget! As with Britain, such massive costs threaten the Navy financially, for half its shipbuilding budget is being spent on this one ship alone. General Dynamics is building the Trident in Groton, Connecticut. But the major missile contractor is Lockheed. Over 25 other companies, including Westinghouse, GE, RCA and IBM have current contracts. Congressional hawks have many brokers among their constituents.

Finally, we come to the Cruise missile, which recalls a sinister memory for the British people, who – unlike the Americans – sat for ten months under the Nazis' V1 and V2 onslaught from the occupied Netherlands, serviced so well by a certain Wernher von Braun, before his promotion to a more honourable spot in the US rocket service. (Except that the Cruise missile will leave behind it, not just a crumbled housing block – as one saw in London streets – but a desolation wider than Hiroshima and Nagasaki combined!)

The Cruise missile is a small, subsonic, pilotless aeroplane, 14 to 20 feet long. It flies at tree-top level, eluding enemy radar, guiding itself to the target by means of a tiny computer which is supposed to match terrain features against computerized maps. It is relatively cheap and can be launched from almost any vehicle on land, sea or in the air. Yet Cruise missiles are expected to carry large warheads to within 100 feet of the target.

Critics have warned that Cruise missiles, like the neutron

40

bomb, could lower the 'nuclear threshold' and make nuclear war more likely and 'thinkable', because they *look* less forbidding than a huge ballistic missile. Thefts and accidents would also be a risk if the missiles were dispersed widely. It is a perfect godsend to terrorists! Nations with a 'nuclear capability' could use versions of the Cruise missile as delivery systems for nuclear bombs so that, by the end of the century, a dozen countries could have them cheaply – mass-produced mass-murderers. A short-term American advantage could thus turn into a perilous long-term liability for everyone.

Safety questions have already been raised about this venomous missile, designed to duck below enemy radar and weave its way 1,000 miles over varied terrain to deliver a nuclear warhead. However, in December 1979, an unarmed missile weaved instead into a hillside in California and another veered into a cattle range. Both had been fired from a B-52 bomber about 400 miles off the California coast; both missiles were supposed to end up at a Utah test site. Three of five offshore launches crashed (one dropped into the ocean) and, in all, seven missiles had gone down out of the 16 in aircraft-launched tests.

These crashes raised questions not only about the effectiveness of the Cruise missile, but also about the safety of citizens living near its test path. (*Herald Tribune*, 4 January 1980). When Shakespeare warned: 'Put not your trust in princes,' he might have added 'nor generals'. In this case General Dynamics might be appropriately listed, as the three offshore mislaunches had come from their workshops. (We might recall President Carter's helicopters caught in an Iranian sandstorm!)

Boeing and General Dynamics are currently building competing versions of the Cruise missile for the US Air Force and Navy – and for faithful NATO. A 'flyoff' between the two was scheduled in 1979. McDonnell Douglas are working on the guidance system, and Williams Research Corporation hold a contract for Cruise missile engines. Many other companies will be involved. *If* the weapon goes into serious production.

The Cruise missiles that NATO proposes to station in Britain from 1983 may be housed on two of the seven existing US Air Force bases. The individual missile launchers are mobile, so if war even *threatened* – or another six-minute 'red alert' is sprung – they would be scattered across the countryside. But to minim-

41

ize the environmental impact of this (to the British) too nostalgic weapon, the deployment plans now being prepared in the Ministry of Defence, envisage concentrating them in two or three locations. Suggested areas are Lakenheath in Suffolk and Upper Heyford in Oxfordshire, because USAF F.111 bombers, armed with nuclear weapons, already operate from there.

Fortunately, there is a growing vocal opposition in Britain to these super-sized V1s and V2s. For example, 88 university faculty members wrote to *The Times* on 13 February 1980 in these specific terms:

> The likelihood of a nuclear war is now greater than at any time since October 1962. Both the super-powers have contributed to this terrifying state of affairs: the Soviet Union by its intervention in Afghanistan, the United States by its proposed installation of a 'new generation' of nuclear weapons in Europe.
>
> Neither event is irreversible, and while we can actively press for Soviet withdrawal from Afghanistan we can also repudiate the Brussels agreement to station Cruise missiles on British soil. These missiles multiply the lethal dangers of accident or miscalculation, make a 'local' or 'theatre' nuclear war the more likely, and make it especially likely that this country will be a target in such a war.
>
> We, the undersigned, appeal to the Government to keep Cruise missiles out of the United Kingdom.

The signatories also state that 'should the Government refuse to do so, we urge the British people to join us in contesting the installation of such missiles'. This is the voice of democracy. This is the voice of reason. As it is echoed in more and more countries, this weight of added fear will be lifted from people's minds.

The trend towards qualitative improvements is going to continue, however, as long as new weapons can replace old ones. The current scandal of NATO's acceptance of 572 'upgraded' warheads for the 1980s has yet to be appreciated by a gullible public. But the US had promised to start negotiating SALT III as soon as the Senate had completed SALT II: next time striving both for force *reductions* and for an end to the technological

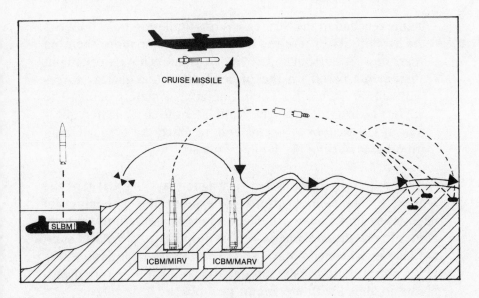

Fig. 5   The threat from land, sea and air.
Source: UNESCO Courier

arms race. SALT II *could* thus provide momentum for reaching
these goals in SALT III. But strong public pressure is essential
to encourage such initiatives.

The 1980s plan to upgrade NATO's European missile force
has been blamed, as we noticed, on Russia's deployment of the
SS-20, a new rocket capable of striking targets throughout
Western Europe from mobile bases in the Soviet Union. The
572 new NATO weapons are American-owned and operated,
and are being produced to the usual refrain: to prevent the
creation of a 'military imbalance'. In NATO eyes, however,
America's (somewhat suspect) commitment to defend Europe
will be more credible, it is argued, now that its 'forward'
weapons are not on *American* soil, which the US might be
hesitant to use for fear of retaliation against its own heartland.
Yet their presence, parked beside East Anglian motorways,
would be a reminder of what America's *British* shield would
suffer in even a 'limited' nuclear war.

These new proposals [points out the Committee for a Sane
Nuclear Policy, Washington] undermine the spirit of agree-

ments reached in the Strategic Arms limitation talks between the United States and the Soviet Union. For more than ten years now, American and Soviet negotiators have worked out agreements based on the principle that the nuclear forces they aim at each other should be approximately equal. The Soviets have agreed to leave until later the complicated question of US weapons systems able to reach the Soviet Union from bases *outside* the United States.

The military balance is not so fragile (says SANE) that the United States cannot afford to explore the possibility of negotiating limits on *new* nuclear weapons. And, in the light of Soviet President Brezhnev's recent proposal at a WAPO summit held in Warsaw in May 1980 to *begin* such negotiations, the US is obligated to pursue mutual arms reduction before deciding to go ahead with any major new plans.

Meantime, Professor Richard Pipes of Harvard University has stated: 'the Soviet military take the prospect of strategic war with the United States seriously, and they are developing what is known as a "war-fighting" and "war-winning" strategy for it. This evidence, of course, has considerable bearing on our own strategic posture in general, and on our approach to SALT in particular.' This reasoning seems incontrovertible, if we study in depth the development of Russian 'defence' policy since World War II. It is the US that is calling the tune, however, though insisting that it is all a reaction to Moscow.

Nonetheless, what we are more concerned with in this book is not to praise the folly of Moscow, but to ask whether the West has no wiser strategy of its own? There can be no doubt that the NATO decision in November 1979 to hit the jack-pot with these 572 'upgraded' weapons will leave the Russians little choice but to pursue their own suicidal policy to beat the winner.

This 'beat the winner' mentality has now disastrously pervaded both sides. First, Moscow's brutal and ill-judged invasion of Afghanistan brought not only a rude shock to their self confidence about 'détente', but more significantly an unexpectedly strong UN General Assembly condemnation of 104 votes, to only 18 against and 18 abstentions. But, second, Carter's intricate counter-move to placate his own backwoodsmen – to switch the seat of the 1980 Olympic Games – could hardly have revealed more pitifully the mess that the arms race has brought upon bewildered statesmen! The whole purpose and ethics of this traditionally recurring event, involving all countries and peoples, is thus perverted and debased by being dragged into the NATO/WAPO cockpit.

But perhaps that final degradation is because the modern revival of the Olympic Games has already for years been exploited as a showpiece of tribal egotism and national glorification. Our television screens are resplendent with national flags and martial anthems sung *ad nauseam*, not to the glory of the individual champions (as Pindar did in timeless verse over two millennia ago), but to the governments which sponsor and finance them. Thus, an ancient festival of joy has become a modern theatre of chauvinism. ('Thrash the Russians' read a spectator's billboard at the Lake Placid Winter Games in February 1980.)

What a chance was missed, in this atmosphere of inter-state bickering and military rivalry, not to respond when the Prime Minister of Greece proposed that the Games come back to their neutral homeland? (Greece had sensibly refused in 1980 to rejoin NATO's integrated military structure.) What a moral lesson the Games have to teach our cruelly divided world, which has reduced the individual to a mathematically insignificant target for a Cruise missile or Backfire bomber!

It was the *individual* who won in the glory of his manhood; his crown of laurel had no economic worth. For a thousand years, beginning in 776 BC, the poets and dramatists of the whole Mediterranean world emblazoned his name in gold for posterity. The Games were, in fact, religious festivals. A Truce of God was proclaimed if wars between the city states coincided with them. Not only field events, but music and drama, sculpture and dancing – all the friendly arts –brought the cream of Hellenic culture together into a universal ceremonial, where the gods were the most honoured spectators.

Must we rely, as we approach the 21st century, on the same martial slogans and nationalistic anthems that emerged along with the sovereign states and greedy empires of the 18th and 19th centuries? Is there not richer music that 'We the peoples' can join *together* in? For example, Beethoven's Ninth 'Ode to

45

Joy' or in the United Nations anthem that world citizen Pablo Casals has composed? In calling the Olympics back home to Greece, a former British athlete, Christopher Brasher, tells of his own vision, far beyond the cold-warmongers of the 1980s when he writes: 'They carried no flags, they represented no nation, no ideology, no political system. Each was an individual, entire unto himself ... These individuals spoke many languages, but they understood one another, for they spoke the common language of sport.' (*Observer*, 3 February 1980).

(4) Non-proliferation at risk

In a decision on 3 August 1978 that could affect thousands of former soldiers, the US Veterans' Appeals Board decided to award service-connected disability benefits to an Army veteran suffering from leukaemia, who claimed that his illness resulted from exposure to radiation during 1957 nuclear weapons tests. He was one of 300,000 servicemen who took part in nuclear weapons tests in Nevada or in the Pacific between 1948 and 1958. Other soldiers were witnesses to nuclear explosions. Moreover, according to the *Washington Post*, about 2,400 former soldiers, who participated in the tests, reported to the Defense Department that they had subsequently become ill either with leukaemia or some other form of cancer.

The Veterans' Appeals Board found that 'it is reasonably probable' that the radiation exposure during the 1957 weapons test, called 'Smoky', was a competent causative factor of disease, even though the leukaemia appeared many years after exposure and after the veteran's retirement from service.

The cases of Donald Coe and of Paul Cooper, another ex-GI at the Smoky test, have been the first to focus public interest on a connection between low-level radiation exposure of nuclear test participants and subsequent development of leukaemia and other forms of cancer. Mr Cooper died of leukaemia in February 1978.

The 'peaceful' uses of nuclear energy fall beyond the scope of this book, but Dr Keith Suter of the University of Sydney makes another relevant point: 'In the continuing search for new dimensions in terror, for new vulnerabilities and pressure points, terrorists may find an unexpected ally in the growing nuclear power industry. Special nuclear materials and facilities offer terrorists the potential for considerable political leverage. Indeed, already nuclear installations have been attacked.' (*Uranium, the Law and You*, 1978).

This brings us, again, to consider the steps now being taken in the broader political field by the UN. The Non-proliferation Treaty (NPT) of 1968 to stop 'proliferation' of nuclear weapons, sets up safeguards against even assumed 'peaceful' uses of the perilous atom. Alas, the line between war use and peace use is becoming an increasingly thin one!

Britain is to start producing its own highly enriched uranium in 1980, suitable for use in nuclear weapons. A special plant will be built for the Ministry of Defence by British Nuclear Fuels at Capenhurst, Cheshire, subject to planning permission. The purpose of the new facility is allegedly to produce fuel suitable for the propulsion of the Navy's nuclear-powered submarines. But it is arguable that the Government is considering a new generation of nuclear weapons for the 1990s.

Uranium in its natural state contains only 0.71 per cent of the isotope U-235. It has to be enriched until it contains about 4.5 per cent for civil power plants – or about 97 per cent for nuclear weapons. The Ministry has given several reasons for the sudden decision to switch to a home-made product. The main reason would seem to be the Navy's growing number of nuclear-powered submarines. But outside experts think that the Ministry, in the long term, is more interested in making Britain's nuclear weapons programmes less dependent upon the United States.

The International Atomic Energy Agency (IAEA) has the central responsibility for keeping the war/peace line intact. As a result of safeguards agreements under the NPT, the Agency's safeguard coverage today is very extensive. There are only five states in the world, besides the nuclear-weapon states, that have significant nuclear activities *not* subject to Agency safeguards, namely: Egypt, India, Israel, South Africa and Spain. Nevertheless, any state that is not a party to NPT or the Tlatelolco Treaty is free to build or otherwise acquire unsafeguarded nuclear plant. The NPT requires each non-nuclear weapon state party to conclude a safeguards agreement with this UN Agency, covering all of the state's peaceful nuclear activities. Fifty-five states have wisely done so and have safeguards agreements in force.

Small concessions to the new international order are thus steadily being made all the time. An agreement between the United Kingdom, the European Atomic Energy Community (EURATOM) and the International Atomic Energy Agency (IAEA) for the application of safeguards in the United Kingdom under the Treaty, entered into force on 17 July 1978. By the terms of the agreement, the IAEA has the right to apply safeguards on sources of special fissionable material in nuclear facilities in the United Kingdom, subject only to exclusions for national security reasons. (The UK decides, of course, *what* the latter are!)

The spill-over of the nuclear weapons business is too complicated for us to follow here. But those retired generals who still envisage World War III wearing World War II uniforms, might consider the *known* biological effects of ionizing radiation on human beings, even beyond the scope of their 'defensive' weapons. There is growing alarm that hundreds of thousands of persons may risk cancer from exposure to smaller doses of radiation than had previously been considered harmful.

For example, the US Government restricts workers' annual radiation exposure to five rems, long believed to have been a safe limit. (Five rems equals more than 166 chest X-rays.) But scientists and Congress are now reassessing the occupational exposure limit. Several recent disclosures have raised a warning flag, because the cancer victims involved were supposedly exposed to less than five rems a year.

A study of naval shipyard workers in Portsmouth, New Hampshire, has suggested that the nation's 36,400 nuclear submarine workers have six times more chance of developing leukaemia than the general population. Again, at least eight cases of leukaemia have been reported among the former military men involved in nuclear bomb test blasts between 1945 and 1962. Reports of harm to people employed in nuclear power plants will surely exacerbate fear of the plants to nearby communities. And then there are also Three Mile Island risks.

And what of the terrorist who imagines he can somehow cow or 'control' his government, in the same way that the more sophisticated hawks imagine that they can stop communism or liquidate capitalism by a few well-placed warheads? And there are constant dangers to human rights, implicit in the development of nuclear power, particularly from fast-breeder reactors leading to a 'plutonium economy'. A plutonium bomb could be made from a few kilograms of plutonium, a material which can safely be handled with rubber gloves. Extraordinary precautions would have to be taken to prevent this material getting into the hands of 'civilian' terrorists.

Professor Alan F. Westin has stated in a report published by the Office of Technology Assessment of Congress: 'As incidents of non-nuclear terrorism have mounted world-wide, and as assaults have been made on nuclear facilities in several countries by various radical groups, there has been an increased program to safeguard such facilities from actions such as sabotage and deliberate release of radioactive materials.' Excellent advice! Why should not governments institute a programme to safeguard all of us from the infinitely greater terrorism of the nuclear arms race?

In 1980, the second five-year review conference of the nuclear Non-proliferation Treaty is scheduled in Geneva. It is unlikely that the 107 signatories have found much cause for self-congratulation. An assessment from the Swedish International Peace Research Institute (SIPRI) runs: 'NPT is gradually being eroded, mainly because of the inconsistent policies of the nuclear material *suppliers* and the non-fulfilment of the disarmament obligations undertaken by the nuclear weapons Powers.'

The most important clause of the 1968 Treaty declares that countries possessing nuclear weapons should not transfer them to anyone else. But by weapons the treaty means warheads, not their delivery systems. This type of vagueness has made the proliferation issue very easy to undermine. Non-nuclear powers wishing to purchase nuclear technology have to accept safeguards laid down by the NPT, and these safeguards include having their installations inspected by teams from the IAEA, as indicated above.

So there are two kinds of violation. One is *vertical* proliferation, whereby the superpowers increase their own arsenals. Then there is *horizontal* proliferation – the acquisition of nuc-

49

lear warheads by nations that previously had none. Third World countries without nuclear weapons have recently had some bad examples set them by such non-signatories as Israel and South Africa. (The names of these two countries were also linked together when a mysterious explosion took place in the Southern Indian Ocean in 1979.) But undoubtedly the first major setback to NPT took place on 18 May 1974 when India exploded a 15 kiloton device. The plutonium for this test had been acquired by circumventing restrictions imposed by the Canadians, who sold them a powerful research reactor, not subject to IAEA safeguards. Indian nuclear engineers then produced their own fuel, claiming that the Canadian fuel was their own.

It was noted above that India is not a signatory of NPT. Since US policy has – until the Afghan crisis – been to prevent the spread of atomic weapons *horizontally*, uranium shipments to India have been held up, to the consternation of the Indian nuclear planners. But to remove this source of limitation, while seeking Delhi's co-operation against Russia's invasion, President Carter gave the green light in May 1980 for 38 tons of enriched uranium to be shipped to Tarapur nuclear power station north of Bombay. Whether this is or is not a violation of the US Non-proliferation Act is now in the lap of Congress and the Nuclear Regulatory Commission.

It is getting more difficult for other countries not to join the nuclear club. Pakistan is well on the way to having its first test. President Zia ul-Haq (just like the Indians) has insisted that his programme is for peaceful purposes. Moreover, other Muslim states have been trying to acquire nuclear weapons to match the arsenal of atomic bombs that Israel is widely assumed to have manufactured out of a shipload of stolen uranium.

So the race goes on. Fridtjof Nansen, the Arctic explorer, humanitarian and founder of the world's first refugee organization, once said: 'Though statesmen appear to their own people as moral men, when it comes to relations between nations, they act like a den of thieves.'

(5) How World War III might begin

Although old-fashioned generals would prefer World War III to begin at the eastern frontier of NATO to suit the expectation of the NATO war games, the event would be likely to be different. Some non-aligned world leaders are speculating, in fact, that World War III has already begun and that it has begun in their territories, where the big powers are now sparring for position. Even Iranian women were being trained to expect an invasion in 1980. But the invasion occurred next door!

Singapore's foreign minister, Sinnthamby Rajaratnam, told the 110-member Conference of Non-Aligned Nations at Belgrade in July 1978, that they should unite and block the nuclear giants from skirmishing on *their* territory. ('Workers of the Third World unite, you have nothing to lose but your wars!') He pointed out that the 'nuclear balance of terror', following World War II, had *ruled out* Europe and North America as the battleground of a third world war. So the threat had been moved to other areas of the globe that had more or less been spared the first two wars. A plague-on-both-your-houses policy was therefore the most sensible way to prevent it from ever beginning.

Yet World War III might not begin in the Third World at all. 'The danger of war by accident . . . grows as modern weapons become more complex, command and control difficulties increase, and the premium is on ever-faster reaction.' This was the verdict of Dean Rusk, US Secretary of State, as long ago as 1962. And it can start any day of the week with someone's brainstorm. The *Guardian* reported (9 October 1975) that one young officer of the US base at Omaha, Nebraska, put it this way: 'We have two tasks. The first is not to let people go off their rockers. That's the negative side. The positive one is to ensure that people act without moral compunction.'

Dr John Cox comments in a recent book (*Overkill*, 1977) on this attitude:

Imagine being cooped up in a submarine for three months on end, never seeing daylight and sleeping next to weapons of mass destruction. Such conditions are not normal and they can create special psychiatric problems. Similarly, those who man missile silos go down into the bowels of the earth each day to check missiles whose purpose is to kill thousands of people at the press of a button. These men undergo regular psychiatric checks and often become disturbed mentally.

A New York psychiatrist, Dr Jonathan Serxner, has investigated the mental state of Polaris submarine crews. Despite lectures, classes, cinema shows and other entertainments, religious services and a library, he found feuds and various minor psychiatric disturbances. About one in twenty of the men needed treatment. There was a chief petty officer who, after five weeks at sea, had delusions of persecution and heard voices. He was given heavy sedation and later transferred from the submarine service.

Nor is it only the people in charge of the missiles and submarines that could cause an inadvertent nuclear explosion, Dr Cox asserts. Thousands of tactical nuclear weapons are scattered around Europe under the control of field commanders. Although their working conditions are not as claustrophobic as those of the submarine and missile silo crews, they also can suffer mental disorders. In 1972 a homesick US pilot climbed into a bomber aircraft at an H-bomb base in East Anglia, flew off and crashed in the English Channel, 'pursued' by other American Air Force planes.

And it is not just the men subjected to these appalling conditions of stress who are in the psychological firing line. Lord Montgomery wrote in a professional Services journal: 'if we are attacked, we use nuclear weapons in our defence. That is agreed; the only proviso is that the politicians have to be asked first. That might be a bit awkward, of course, and personally I would use the weapon first and ask afterwards.'

Then an early 'warning' might turn out to be the real thing. The whole of the North Pole and Arctic is one network of sophisticated gadgets, any one of which may go wrong. Cases are on record where a moon echo has been interpreted as a Soviet movement of missiles and a flight of geese going to warmer climes for the winter has been mistaken for a hostile fighter bomber. These are small – some might say ridiculous – errors, but what used to be called 'national security' now rests on flights of imagination in insecure individuals who, in normal relationships, would be treated as moonstruck and therefore to be avoided at all costs.

Freud had a good deal to say about this fetish called 'national security' – a thinly disguised death-wish conveniently transferred on to the 'enemy'. 'Throughout the life of the individual,' he wrote in *Civilization, War and Death*, 'there is a constant replacement of the external compulsion by the internal.'

Professor Norman O. Brown in *Life Against Death*, says:

It is a shattering experience for anyone seriously committed to the Western traditions of morality and rationality to take a steadfast, unflinching look at what Freud has to say. It is humiliating to be compelled to admit the grossly seamy side of so many grand ideas . . . Freud was right: our real desires are unconscious. It also begins to be apparent that mankind, unconscious of its real desires and therefore unable to obtain satisfaction, is hostile to life and ready to destroy itself. [And he adds:] Freud was right in positing a death instinct, and the development of weapons of destruction makes our present dilemma plain: we either come to terms with our unconscious instincts and drives – with life and with death – or else we surely die.

The biggest of our modern fantasies, perhaps, is the belief that 'military intelligence' *is* intelligent. Just fancy that we should have once entrusted our safety, or our victory in war, to Philby, Burgess, and Maclean! The spate of books that have appeared recently – for James Bond still makes popular newsprint – on the past antics of these men have also revealed that such cloak-and-dagger period pieces are *still* an essential part of our Foreign Office and MI6 diplomatic scenarios. Will it take another 20 years for the grotesque network of lies and spies and mutual deceit that bolsters our arms race to be revealed as the best financed tragi-comedy of the 1980s?

Commenting on World War II's propaganda techniques – now explicitly condemned and prohibited in a dozen UN and UNESCO conventions – the historian A. J. P. Taylor writes in a recent review: 'The press was manipulated or at any rate directed. Wireless stations kept up a ceaseless flow of everything from straight news to deliberate deceptions. The operators of propaganda came near to believing that they could win the war all on their own, and many outsiders shared this curious belief.'

The two most astonishing curiosities of our present cold-war window-dressing machine, however, are firstly that it is the enemy's successes that are boosted up to frighten us, while our own failures are featured most abjectly; and, secondly, that this propaganda-in-reverse is not directed against the enemy (for he has surely a surfeit of his own) but against our own citizens. So the common people, whose taxes support it, lose on both the swings and the roundabouts.

As David Halberstam, a former *New York Times* journalist, points out: 'There is an unwritten law of American journalism that states that the greater and more powerful the platform, the more carefully it must be used and the more closely it must adhere to the norms of American society, particularly the norms of the American Government.' Thus, much of the American media have kept pace with the politicians over such major calamities as McCarthyism, segregation and Vietnam, when a much more detached and critical relationship would have saved many lives, as well as the nation's peace of mind.

Do we expect to find these faithful camp-followers, then, exposing the arms race? No! The American press, with rare exceptions, presents a built-in segment of the arms race itself. Every passing crisis – Angola, Ethiopia, Iran, Afghanistan – is dealt with in terms of pressing *military* response and brazen power politics. Diplomatic correspondents fall over themselves explaining what the *next* military moves should be. So the public always expects the worst. After all, what have the writers to lose? No one reads last month's columns; but they have planted their poison of fear and bellicosity in the public mind. It seems at times almost futile for UN appeals and UNESCO declarations to deplore and condemn national war propaganda and biased news reporting, while the average citizen is being fed daily with the worst of all worlds and a mental conditioning of fear and apprehension.

Again, there are the earth's spark-plug danger spots. Do we need any stronger warning than was presented on our television screens early in 1980, when masses of screaming 'students' were day after day marching through the streets of Teheran and other cities with clenched fists yelling abuse and defiance, not

54

merely at their deposed Shah (who was, in part, responsible for their rage) and the United States, but even at the UN and its Secretary-General?

In other words, the sparks that could ignite World War III spring today, not only from the cynical machinations of foreign offices, but from the uncontrollable chaos of internal disruption in a second or third rate power, that has neither the purpose nor means to commit external aggression. The invasion of Russian forces into Iran's close neighbour – and Washington's 'gut' response – should also warn us that the arms race could guarantee that once East/West war begins – however 'incidental' the cause or pretext – nothing can hold back the holocaust. Disarmament must begin *NOW* and build into a world campaign until this powder-train can no longer be ignited by an 'accident'.

The Afghanistan invasion highlights, too, how vulnerable are the US concepts of its manifest destiny across the globe. President Carter in Washington delivered yet another stern warning to the Soviet Union: 'Let our position be absolutely clear,' he said. 'An attempt by any outside force to gain control of the Persian Gulf region will be regarded as an assault on the vital interests of the United States. *It will be repelled by any means necessary, including military force.*' Evidently the United States now regards the Gulf area, like Western Europe, Japan and the North Pole as falling under its private defence umbrella! And what do the Russians think?

Frontier clashes also continue between Angola and South Africa, which attempted to foul up the negotiated steps in both Namibia and Zimbabwe towards their .non-racial statehood. And several Arabian Gulf states, destabilized by the Iran and Afghanistan incidents, are seeking a common Muslim policy opposing the US pretensions in the Middle East, especially over Israel. Then China is already a nuclear weapon state; while India hesitates to produce a nuclear arsenal because of Pakistan, who might immediately follow suit, if backed by the US.

And, finally, when asked recently what was the implication of US nuclear weapons *remaining* in South Korea, President Carter answered that the implication was that they would be used 'in case of necessity'. Did 'necessity' mean '*if* North Korea committed any aggression against South Korea?' (This was before President Park was assassinated.)

Mr Carter did not suggest that he meant 'only in case of *nuclear* aggression'. Yet he could have been interpreted as saying that, from now on, the US would be the *first* to use nuclear weapons against an ally of the Soviet Union, i.e. North Korea, if the US deemed that military aggression were committed even by a non-nuclear power using only conventional weapons. And even, we might add, if the conventional aggression were not committed against America but against any one of its many allies, large or small, around the globe. President Carter confirmed that he did mean exactly that in the course of his first policy speech before the General Assembly of the United Nations on 4 October 1977: 'I hereby solemnly declare on behalf of the United States that we will not use nuclear weapons except in self-defense; that is, in circumstances of an actual nuclear *or conventional* attack on the United States, our territories or armed forces, or such an attack *on our allies.*' (*New York Times*, 5 October 1977).

The secret illnesses of statesmen can be more dangerous than their secret diplomacy. A Frenchman has written a book on 'The Sick Men who Govern Us' and he selects his specimens from two or three decades ago. But who can truly size up the Sick Men of the Nuclear Age? In the area of most potentially perilous conflicts today – the Middle East – where religious fanaticism is compounded with tribal chauvinism, well-founded rumours have been emerging that 400 pounds of stolen uranium has found its way into Israel's secret arsenal.

There is an increasing anxiety in Western and Eastern governments alike, and also in the Third World, to seek a peaceful long-term solution through the United Nations in the interests of *all* the parties involved in the Arab-Israeli conflict. This must be obvious to every thinking person. But does the stolen uranium encourage this kind of solution? Does it add to anyone's security?

Beneath all these speculations on the 'unknowable' – the accidents of 'things' – lies the immaturity of man, as man. The mere fact that brains and formal education and specialized training are being deliberately misemployed to devise ever more elaborate means to outwit or to counter massacre devices of an assumed enemy calls for a new order of 'peace intelligence' of urgent and exceptional quality.

II
Conventional Killers

(1) New generations of weapons

The term 'conventional', like other military shorthand, covers a vast range of weapons causing unnecessary human suffering, and which have long been prohibited by international law. We might start off with a few, though it is rather an unpleasant subject.

Belligerents in modern warfare are today using weapons which inflict agonizing and terrible suffering. These are quite apart from the nuclear weapons, described in Chapter I, whose radiation causes either death or awesome diseases. Our modern armoury includes incendiary weapons, containing napalm and phosphorus, which produce dreadful burning; and also fragmentation and cluster bombs.

The latest generation of the latter consists of bombs containing pellets of plastic, which, having penetrated the human body, cannot be traced by X-ray. The Swedish delegate at a Conference of Government Experts on the Reaffirmation and Development of International Humanitarian Law Applicable in Armed Conflicts held in Geneva, on 4 May 1972, described this weapon in the following terms:

This is a bouncing anti-personnel mine filled with fifteen pounds of plasticized white phosphorus. When activated, the main part of the mine is propelled about four metres into the air where it explodes, spewing burning white phosphorus in all directions with a radius of about 25 metres. The phosphorus has the quality of gluing to the body when burning, and cannot be scraped off, but must be cut out, leaving frightful wounds. Furthermore, it is highly toxic, poisoning the liver, the kidneys and the nervous system after absorption through the wound.*

Atrocious wounds are caused by hypervelocity rifles, whose bullets become unstable on impact, tumbling in the wound and producing a large cavity. One of these is a bullet fired by the US M.16 rifle, which was described by an Australian surgical team as follows:

Case 1: A Vietnamese civilian was brought in dead after receiving a single projectile from an M.16 in the right thigh. Autopsy showed that the bullet had torn its way through the obturator foramen and disintegrated in the abdomen, only fragments of about 0.5 mm being recovered. Within the abdomen it had wrenched the whole small bowel from its mesentery and had perforated the pancreas, stomach and spleen. Such an injury is comparable to that produced by an explosive missile.

Case 2: A Vietnamese civilian running away from an American received seven shots in the leg, the buttock, the chest and the arm. The injuries outside the abdomen were minor, but several bullets must have penetrated the buttock, leaving a hole in the sacrum which accepted a fist. The rectum was transected and the small bowel perforated in eight places. Once more no trace of the projectiles could be found at laparotomy.†

It will be noted that these two cases refer to *civilians*. There were untold thousands like them, left behind to suffer after the heroes had returned home. But we can well ask: what existing

*Cited in A. Cassese, *Rivista di Diritto Internazionale*, 1975
†Dudley, 'Civilian Battle Casualties in South Vietnam', *British Journal of Surgery*, 5, 1968

legal restraints have been imposed on these categories of cruel weapons? Specific bans have either developed as rules of customary law, or were formulated in treaty provisions that have later passed into customary international law. These prohibitions are therefore applicable to all members of the international community. We can list here only a few of them.

Customary rules have developed ever since the early 1800s specifying that poisoned bullets, projectiles filled with glass and caustic lime, minced lead and chain-bullets are to be proscribed among 'civilized peoples' because they caused needless suffering. Specific prohibitions are embodied in the St Petersburg Declaration of 1868 on explosive projectiles under 400 grams weight. Article 23(a) of the 1899 and 1907 Hague Regulations on Land Warfare prohibited poison or poisoned weapons. The 1899 Hague Declaration on expanding 'dum-dum' bullets and the 1899 Hague Declaration on asphyxiating and deleterious gases were supplemented by the 1925 Geneva Protocol. The 1899 and 1907 Hague Regulations on Land Warfare specifically stated that 'it is especially forbidden . . . to employ arms, projectiles or material which are such as to cause superfluous injury'.

We are now approaching the 21st century, but 'superfluous injury' has become an accepted principle of national foreign policy. Two UN conferences were held in Geneva in 1977 and 1979 to attempt to draft a Convention prohibiting these weapons designed to cause 'unnecessary' injury and suffering. The ostensible purpose of shooting the enemy's soldiers was to put them out of action. But these fiendish weapons are now being made *and intended* to cause torture and death by horrible suffering. These recent Geneva Conferences, dominated by military advisers of 100 governments, adjourned without having agreed on a Convention. But 1980 will see a further session. Does the public care if nothing is done?

The swift approach of the 21st century does not rule out in the military mind the possible resort to a favourite elimination device of the Borgias, namely, *poison*. Deadly poisons, including enough shellfish toxin to kill thousands of people, were recently found in a secret cache maintained by the CIA. Senator Frank Church revealed that the CIA kept both the shellfish toxin and a smaller amount of cobra venom 'in direct contravention' of presidential orders. The Senator said he would eventually find out who in the CIA was responsible, and promised that his Senate Committee on Intelligence Operations would hold public hearings on the matter in spite of White House objections.

These poisons were reportedly developed for the CIA under the code name of 'Project Naomi' during the 1950s. Senator Church said that he had no reason to think any of the toxins were actually used, but that his Committee was investigating 'one particular mission' that apparently never came to fruition, because the object of it was assassinated by other means. He was familiar with an allegation that some toxin was sent to Africa to kill Congolese Premier Patrice Lumumba in 1961, but that the shipment did not arrive in time!

A bigger shock ran through the United States when television viewers in September 1975 actually watched a US Army private trying unsuccessfully to cover an obstacle course while under the influence of a chemical code-named BZ. The soldier could not make his arms reach parallel bars to cross a stream, or even walk through a line of trees without bumping into them.

This film, shown by the Pentagon on the CBS Walter Cronkite show, was shot at the Army's chemical warfare centre at Edgewood Arsenal, Maryland. Since 1953 the centre has apparently carried out experiments on nearly 7,000 servicemen, using agents ranging from LSD to lethal nerve gases. Public anger was aroused and Congressional hearings revealed that the Army never told its 'guinea-pigs' what was being tested on them. It was reported that there was no 'after-care' programme. Three people are known to have died during the experiments, with, as yet, no explanation in two cases. Several others experienced a 'flashback phenomenon' of deep depression, which led to at least two attempted suicides.

It should be emphasized that President Nixon offered the destruction of biological weapons in 1969 following the signing by the US of the International Treaty limiting biochemical warfare. But it was recently disclosed, as noted above, that the CIA had kept two containers of poison – extracted from shellfish and cobra venom – in a warehouse at Fort Dietrick, Maryland.

It was for biological experiments before that ban, however, that the Army recruited 2,000 Seventh Day Adventists who, as conscientious objectors because of their beliefs, had opted to go to the Army medical training centre at Fort Sam, Houston, Texas. They were given a briefing session by the director of the Army Medical Research Institute of Infectious Diseases, and 95 per cent of those briefed volunteered as guinea-pigs. The exact nature of the substances tested on them is not known, but those who declined to join the testing became medical orderlies, and many were sent to Vietnam.

The Soviet Union attempted to influence (then) President Nixon in 1969 to halt *all* chemical and biological weapons development. They have pressed for this ever since, as UN records show. Their technique then was, it seems, to transmit information through double agents working for the FBI. The aim of the agents' messages was to persuade Mr Nixon that *if the United States continued its build-up of chemical weapons*, especially nerve gas, the Soviet Union would be compelled to start a 'crash programme' to match US capabilities. Mr Nixon's decision to renounce US use of biological weapons in November 1969 and later to curb chemical weapons in the US arsenal was in any case good on its own merits.

In March 1980, General Bernard Rogers, supreme NATO Commander, urged in a BBC interview in London that the United States should begin 'producing chemical weapons to deter the Kremlin from using them'. Also the Western European Union (a military organization) recommended in May 1980 that 'NATO's chemical weapon stocks should equal the estimated offensive capability of the Warsaw Pact *as a deterrent*'. The absurdity, once again, of this proposed 'balance' of chemical products could hardly be more obvious. Happily, the same report recommends that NATO should 'encourage bilateral and multilateral negotiations to ban the production, stockpiling and use of chemical weapons with adequate verification'. As to what is 'adequate' has held up negotiations for 20 years. National sovereignty – and not merely Russia's – has consistently blocked UN verification measures, since no nation will allow its enemy to probe.

The question of chemical warfare has, in fact, been discussed intermittently at the UN throughout the 1950s and 1960s, usually in conjunction with biological weapons. The argument whether biological and chemical weapons should be dealt with separately was settled in 1971 by a draft Convention on the Prohibition of the Development, Production and Stockpiling of Bacteriological (Biological) and Toxin Weapons and on Their Destruction.

The General Assembly adopted a resolution urging adoption of that Convention. It contains an undertaking by the parties to negotiate an agreement 'on effective measures for the prohibition of the production and stockpiling of chemical weapons and for their destruction', also on measures concerning equipment and means of delivery. There things seem to have stuck. But it came up once more at a Special Geneva Conference in April 1980. Again, the West was dragging its feet. On the last day of this Conference (the author was present) a red herring was dragged across the final proceedings about an alleged exposure of toxic gas materials in a town in Siberia. The Soviet delegate heatedly denied that this was an escape of war-making materials. But the rest was silence and Russian secrecy produced a crop of hysterical assertions.

Professor René Wadlow, a Geneva disarmament specialist, stated:

> A serious presumption exists that poison gas is being used against the hill tribes in Laos and more widely in Cambodia in violation of the spirit of the 1925 Protocol banning use of poison gas. Unfortunately, no dispute-settlement mechanism exists in the Protocol. An investigation carried out by only a single country – no matter how well done or well publicised – will be discounted as politically motivated ... Therefore, what is necessary is the creation by the United Nations of an ad hoc investigation into the complaint of poison gas use in Laos and Cambodia followed by steps to strengthen the 1925 Protocol by the creation of permanent verification and dispute-settlement procedure. (*Herald Tribune*, 31 December 1979).

Vietnam proved to be – since no one could stop it – an ideal 'laboratory' for testing the effectiveness of America's new techniques in (prohibited) chemical warfare. But, strange to relate, its long-term effectiveness on the *invaders*, no less than on the invaded, has only recently come to light in odd places. A statistical study has been completed in Australia, which reveals that one in four of Australian ex-servicemen exposed in Vietnam to the defoliant 'Agent Orange' have fathered deformed children. The national average of one seriously deformed baby in every 1,000 is 250 times lower than the veterans' rate.

The study was carried out on 50 men who suffered from a variety of complaints, which they believed were caused by contact with Agent Orange in Vietnam between 1965 and 1970. The families of the veterans, all living in New South Wales, contain four children with deformed hands, including three cases in which all the fingers of one hand and half the thumb are missing, two with deformed legs, and including one on a baby girl which had to be amputated.

Moreover, 11 of the men who reported deformed babies suffered themselves from extreme nervousness, and ten from a body rash which has been accepted as being linked to Agent Orange. (In New South Wales overall, only one baby in 2,000 usually suffers such deformity.) A research biochemist on foetal deformities for the Sydney-based Children's Medical Research Foundation said that a total of eight gross limb deformities were included in the ex-servicemen's group.

This group's statistics roughly conformed to those more recently compiled in the United States, where 77 birth defects were reported in the families of 538 ex-servicemen exposed to Agent Orange, a wartime code-name for a defoliant which is one of the phenoxy herbicides containing dioxin, and a phenoxy-type drug that is reputed to bind itself directly to the victim's genetic material. (*The Times*, 4 January 1980). The US veterans' protest group has actually called itself 'Agent Orange Victims International'. It contends in its legal claim that the defoliant caused serious maladies in servicemen exposed to it and birth defects in some of their children. So the US Government has begun (in 1980) a long-term study of the defoliant's deleterious health effects. But will they *stop* its use?

Meanwhile, Edmund Juteau, organizer of the campaign to link the herbicide Agent Orange with cancer, died in February 1980 at 30 years of age in a hospital in New Hartford, NY, where he was being treated for cancer. An Air Force staff sergeant in Vietnam in the early 1970s, he said that he had been sprayed with Agent Orange and he had won an appeal from the

Veterans' Administration that his cancer was linked to his duty in Vietnam.

The British Army is, nonetheless, planning for the use of chemical weapons against Russia, even though their use has been banned in Europe since 1925. Officers at the Staff College at Camberley have accordingly been briefed about 'a terrifying chemical armoury built up by the Soviet Union'. They are reported as saying that they would like to see Britain develop a 'deterrent' – according to a BBC television series called 'War School'. (*Observer*, 27 January 1980). Once more we meet the 'balance' or eye-for-an-eye illusion.

A platoon from a British infantry regiment were the first troops to arrive at Porton Down, Wiltshire, to inaugurate NATO's first officially designated battle training area for chemical warfare – just three months ahead of the Geneva Conference convened in March 1980 *to re-confirm the outlawing* of these inhuman and illegal weapons!

The Convention against Bacteriological and Toxic Weapons entered into force on 26 March 1975 after ratification by the 22nd party, including the 'depositaries' of the Convention, namely, the Soviet Union, the United Kingdom and the United States. Some 85 ratifications and 34 signatures have since been deposited. Under article I, states parties undertake,

> never in any circumstances to develop, produce or otherwise acquire or retain:
> Microbial or other biological agents, or toxins whatever their origin or method of production, of types and in quantities that have no justification for prophylactic, protection or other purposes:
> Weapons, equipment or means of delivery designed to use such agents or toxins for hostile purposes or in armed conflict.

And under article II, states parties undertake 'to destroy or to divert for peaceful purposes' all biological agents, toxins, weapons, equipment and means of delivery which are in their possession or under their jurisdiction or control.

When the Review Conference of the parties to the Biological

Weapons Convention met in Geneva in March 1980 the Secretary-General said:

> The significance of the Convention comes into sharper focus when one considers that the unceasing progress in science and technology leads to the development and production of newer and more dangerous weapons. The arresting of this ominous trend at least in one area is an achievement that resulted from long but persevering efforts of the whole international community. It proves the importance of similar efforts in other areas of disarmament.'

Yet, since 1971, the General Assembly has at each of its regular sessions adopted resolutions calling for 'priority' negotiations which would lead to early agreement on a prohibition of all *chemical* weapons. In 1972, Eastern European members submitted a separate draft convention on the prohibition of the development, production and stockpiling of chemical weapons and on their destruction. In recent years, discussions concerning a ban on all chemical warfare have centred on questions related to the verification of compliance with the obligations undertaken by the parties to the future agreement. The scope of a comprehensive convention would, from its inception, extend to all chemical weapons which the parties wished to prohibit, from the stage of their development up to their use, including the means of delivery. Once again, it is political will that is lacking.

Since the worst horrors of science fiction have long been outmoded by what the Pentagon and Kremlin backroom boys have on their drawing-boards, it is no longer a secret that both the United States and the Soviet Union are exploring laser and particle-beam weapons. In fact, in developing these new weapons, the two countries could set off a new phase of the arms race. Laser weapons make a difference in military calculations and their deployment would force adversaries to develop counter-measures or to increase numbers of offensive weapons in order to deal with the improved defensive capability of the laser systems.

The Pentagon has publicly acknowledged that it is studying the possibility of particle-beam weapons, whose high-energy beams of electrons, protons or neutrons would be directed to inflict damage, in order to ensure, they claim: (1) ballistic missiles defence, directed beams being used to hit incoming missiles; (2) satellite-borne anti-satellite killers, being launched in space to attack enemy satellites; and (3) ship-borne and aircraft-borne anti-missile weapons.

Fortunately, the report says that the first feasibility demonstrations of laser weapons will not take place until into the 1980s. Meantime, Soviet negotiators, working with US representatives to seek a common position on radiological weapons, have raised the issue of particle-beam weapons. The Russians urge a ban on their development as weapons that would 'affect biological targets as weapons of mass-destruction'. And the West?

(2) From napalm to radiation

Skin is easily damaged by heat, the degree of damage depending upon the amount of heat. Burn injuries differ from the wounds commonly caused by conventional weapons in the difficulty of their medical treatment. Where medical resources are modest, casualties from napalm have little chance of receiving medical aid. In recent wars – such as the Americans in Vietnam and the Israelis in Lebanon – napalm weapons appear to have produced an exceptionally high proportion of deaths compared with other weapons. Napalm injuries may be intensely painful. Recovery is slow, and the patient remains in great pain. Napalm and white phosphorus burns are likely to leave a victim disfigured for the rest of his life.

Flame-throwers used in World War I have today become weapons of mass-destruction. In fact, incendiary bomb attacks on cities such as Dresden, conducted during World War II, proved almost as destructive as the atomic bombs dropped on Hiroshima and Nagasaki.

Most human beings have an instinctive fear of fire, and the psychological effects of incendiary weapons are commonly listed among their 'attractions' to the military mind. During mass-fires, large numbers of people become trapped by great walls of flame, offering no possibility of escape. And the use of napalm or white phosphorus, which clings to surfaces and to fleeing people while burning, increases the overall psychological impact. With a general breakdown of communications and public services, the result would be panic. Survival procedures become totally ineffective.

Destruction of houses and shelters results in a hostile environment and exposure to the weather, thus increasing overall suffering and loss of life. This situation is likely to be *worse in the developing countries*, for not only will fewer medical resources be available, but widespread malnutrition, chronic anaemias and other deficiencies will increase rapidly on exposure. It is the Third World which will suffer without remedy if the great powers imagine (as some living generals do) that 'their side' could win a conventional war.

But what now of the neutron bomb? This controversial nuclear weapon kills by neutron radiation while minimizing property destruction. *It is being promoted as a battlefield weapon that could make nuclear war more 'thinkable'.* Widespread public opposition in Europe, however, has delayed the US adoption of the neutron bomb. If opposition grows in the US, as it is growing in Europe, the President will probably be forced to stop the bomb being produced.

Officially known as an 'enhanced radiation weapon', it is, in fact, a small 'low yield' nuclear bomb. Its special shielding mechanism reduces the blast effect, but increases the release of radiation energy in the form of neutrons. The blast and heat from the explosion destroy *everything* within 300 yards, and the neutron radiation kills most people within a mile radius. Beyond that distance, the damage diminishes.

It has the same effect on humans as DDT on insects. Neutrons attack the central nervous system, causing immediate nausea, diarrhoea, and convulsions. Depending on the dose, some victims die within hours. For others, death comes 60 to 90 days later with respiratory failure, delirium, or coma. Those not killed would be prone to leukaemia or other cancers in later years.

It is claimed that in the event of an invasion in Europe or elsewhere, the bomb could be used against advancing troops and tanks, while leaving bridges, power plants and other important structures intact. But by introducing this new weapon NATO would send the wrong message to other nations. It contradicts the oft-stated goals of non-proliferation and 'zero nuclear weapons'. Some critics believe, on the contrary, that the neutron bomb lowers the threshold of nuclear war, since military commanders might be more likely to use it than bigger nuclear weapons.

Funds for the neutron bomb were included in the US Department of Energy's 1979 budget. Total cost of production could run as high as $1.5 billion, if the President gives the go-ahead. Will he? One answer was given by Daniel Ellsberg at a recent Rocky Flats, Colorado, anti-nuclear demonstration. He said: 'The neutron bomb is the match to the nuclear oven in which mankind will perish. These demonstrations prove that some of humanity will not go quietly to the crematorium!' This time, holocaust is preventable. But will we?

Radiological weapons would utilize radioactive material to cause vast damage or injury. The potential for such weapons was recognized in fact more than three decades ago. Yet at that time, the amount of highly radioactive material in existence was small. In succeeding years, the accumulation of radioactive material has increased at an accelerating rate and now exists at facilities in more than 50 countries.

The banning of radiological weapons has most fortunately been making progress on the governmental level. The US and the USSR submitted jointly to the Geneva-based Committee on Disarmament in July 1979 a proposed agreement *prohibiting* radiological weapons. The US and the USSR urged that the Committee give their initiative prompt consideration, so that a draft treaty text could be developed. As proposed by the two parties, the treaty would prohibit the development, production, stockpiling, acquisition, or possession of radiological weapons.

Nuclear explosive weapons, alas!, which invariably produce radiation along with their other destructive effects, constitute a category of weapons of mass destruction separate from radiological weapons and so would be *excluded* from coverage by provisions of any radiological weapon treaty. However, we can at least end this section on one note of hopeful achievement for Geneva's new Committee on Disarmament.

(3) Tankology: machines replace men

If neutron weapons are being advocated as the essential means for stopping Russian tanks sweeping through central Europe, then tanks must be pretty formidable gadgets! They certainly are. They are more than formidable. They represent a new and permanent element in 'conventional' war. When the Israeli armour swept through southern Lebanon in March 1978, only 18 *soldiers* were killed; though there were many Lebanese deaths (most of the Palestine exiles in Lebanon having escaped), while nearly a quarter of a million homeless Lebanese civilians fled north to safety, as refugees.

The reason for the extremely low death rate of the invading soldiers, in contrast to the under-protected people whom they attacked, was due to the fact – the TV evidence was clear about this – that the Israelis were all boxed up in machines. The latest design of American tanks – their armour vastly improved since the disastrous Yom Kippur War – and other armoured vehicles rolled unmolested across the Lebanese fields and countryside, as the American-made planes swooped down from the skies. There was not a foot-soldier to be seen.

If this goes on (and the military men expect it to) the old concept of cannon fodder going over the top will become meaningless, except for television replays. In fact, as these new fighting leviathans get more computerized, they will move along the ground and across lakes and rivers, like the Cruise missiles move over the ground. They won't need any drivers or gunners at all. They will be so full of electronics that there won't be room – or need – for mere men inside.

Tanks started in a very modest way. In fact, Julius Caesar knew how useful chariots with cutting edges could be in overwhelming the enemy. British munitions chief Lloyd George took up the tank business seriously at the beginning of World War I, when the tank became a major weapon against the German mass troop assaults.

Since then the tank has become a forward weapon of assault. Its weight, speed and destructive power have made it the spearhead of advance against the enemy. But one other change has taken place since Lloyd George pleaded for his pioneer tanks. This change is so fundamental that it should be set out in capi-

Battle tanks	Weight	Speed	Range	Gun	Crew
T-55	35.7 t	31 mph	250 m	100 mm	4
M60	45.5 t	30 mph	310 m	105 mm	4
T-62	36.6 t	30 mph	250 m	115 mm	4
Leopard	39.5 t	40 mph	375 m	105 mm	4
Heavy Tanks					
T-10	48.2 t	22 mph	135 m	122 mm	4
Chieftain	53.0 t	30 mph	310 m	120 mm	4

Table 2   Tanks: NATO–Soviet Comparison Chart

tals, thus: ALL MODERN WAR WEAPONS ARE OFFEN-SIVE.

There are no 'defensive' weapons any more. They are only called defensive to console the consciences of worried people 'back home'. Every weapon – from the proposed neutron bomb to the leviathan tank – is a weapon of *attack*. This is because defence has disappeared entirely. It has been replaced by deterrence, and deterrence *means* attack, or it means nothing.

A tank is not required to counter another tank. The Middle East War in October 1973 demonstrated the vulnerability of the tank. Both Arabs and Israelis suffered substantial losses of tanks, totalling about 2,000. *Anti-tank* missile technology had by then overcome the best protective counter-measures available. A half-million dollar tank can be destroyed by a very inexpensive, *man-carried* anti-tank weapon such as the $4,000 TOW missile. These developments prompted Colonel Edward B. Atkinson in *Army* magazine to write a tantalizing article entitled: 'Is the Soviet Army Obsolete?' The Soviet Union seems reliant, however, on tanks and tank-dependent tactics that stem nostalgically from World War II. Major-General

70

	Tanks	Towed Artillery	Combat Ships	Submarines	Combat Aircraft	Helicopters	Missiles
US	3,560	785	150	22	1,053	460	10,035
France	440	80	32	2	275	265	520
UK	1,105	5	93	3	105	45	640
Subtotal	5,105	870	275	27	1,433	770	11,195
USSR	5,220	2,550	41	6	1,565	380	3,950
Total	**10,325**	**3,420**	**316**	**33**	**2,998**	**1,150**	**15,145**

Table 3 Major weapons exported by the Big Four, 1971–75 (including deliveries to developing countries, Australia, New Zealand, Japan and South Africa). *Source*: US Arms Control and Disarmament Agency

Howard H. Cooksey, US Army Acting-Deputy Chief of Staff for Research and Development, recently observed that 'certainly in the Mideast war, the Israelis found out the hard way that *blitzkrieg* tactics will not work'.

Tank modifications are going on the whole time, on both sides of the Iron Curtain. No one quite knows in what directions. Commenting on the NATO enigma, the US journal *Science* states that the battle tank is still the principal weapon of a modern army: 'Far from driving the tank into extinction, technological developments such as the anti-tank missile have only hastened its rate of evolution. For the past 15 years, however, the United States has stumbled from one fiasco to another in its attempts to design a new main battle tank, but seems at last to have a winner.' (*Science*, 14 July 1978).

Science goes on to say that both the failure and success of the tank development programme are integrally related to a central crisis of the NATO alliance, i.e. the lack of co-operation in designing, developing, and producing new weapons. Through failure to standardize, NATO allies at present field 31 different anti-tank weapons and seven different tanks! Such diversity

71

causes a formidable logistics problem. It is, therefore, a principal factor in this paradox that the backward economies of the Warsaw Pact can out-produce advanced NATO economics in tanks by a ratio of 4 to 1. The article concludes:

Though everyone agrees on the importance of NATO standardization, the commonly proposed remedies often seem worse than the disease. European countries, already fretful that they buy $8 of military equipment from the United States for every one dollar's worth that they sell, view calls for standardization as another pressure to 'buy American'.

III
War Games for Real

The famous Helsinki Accords of 1975 contained an assortment of minor agreements which are not given much press publicity simply because they are working reasonably well. Although the Final Act is not legally binding, there is a political commitment by the signatory states to give prior notification of major military manoeuvres. These are defined as involving more than 25,000 ground troops. The Final Act also calls for certain specified actions by signatory states, including the exchange of observers to manoeuvres and prior notification of smaller-scale manoeuvres, defined as those having fewer than 25,000 troops.

Five years' experience has demonstrated that all signatory states have generally complied with this provision for prior notification of major military manoeuvres, though some Western observers have complained that they can't see very much. However that may be, we move from present reality, with all its untidiness, into a land of make-believe when a retired English general gives preliminary notification of the third world war, timed to take place in 1985. Unfortunately, he does not stand alone, though he is not in very good company. For Richard Nixon, whom top US historians have called 'the only criminal who occupied the US Presidency', has presented us in his 1980 book, *The Real War*, with his call to a new moral crusade: 'In the war we are fighting – World War III – there is no substitute for victory and a strategy for victory.'

(1) The Hackett Game

True to well-recognized rules that retired generals remain experts at re-fighting their previous war, General Sir John Hackett has produced a terrifying dream-scenario of the next war in his *The Third World War, August 1985* (1978). Not unnaturally his blood-bath for the crucial year 1985 has to begin, according to tradition, in Poland. So we are back in the *blitzkrieg* era once more. World War III is actually sparked in 1985, however, by the ubiquitous US marines landing in Fiume to win Yugoslavia back from the Russians who, at long last, had got so tired of much-revered Tito's neutrality that they attempted a Prague Spring on the soft under-belly of Europe. But the Yanks got there first this time.

Why all this? By August 1985, the Soviet Union faces mounting disaffection among its many national minorities. A good point to start. After 35 years – a whole generation at peace – the leopard is suddenly changing his spots and thinks that a European war would be an improvement on détente. The technological gap and the balance of nuclear terror is all the time growing in the Americans' favour; but the Russians have ground superiority in conventional arms. With the Russian (mistaken) confidence that the Americans will not dare to risk mutual nuclear suicide, the Soviet war machine slides into action on 4 August 1985. A tank invasion of Western Europe is aimed at the destruction of the Atlantic Alliance. What this argument does – though General Hackett does not appreciate what he is doing – is to blow the whole 'deterrence'dogma sky-high.

They quickly come a cropper, however, thanks to the Western lead in electronics. The forces of the Alliance outwit those of the WAPO from scratch. That is the grim story as told by General Sir John Hackett, former Deputy Chief of the General Staff and Commander of NATO's Northern Army Group in Europe. True to the best Hollywood routines, the good guys will beat the bad guys in the end, and quickly – for, unlike World Wars I and II, it lasted only the *expected* few weeks! And Russia had already changed its spots from red to pink by 1986. Sixty years of Bolshevism had gone into reverse in only twelve months!

But it is a tough game while it lasts. Nevertheless, all the

NATO rules are faithfully kept. The nukes don't go into the fray until the battle is on the home ground: Birmingham is eliminated, so is Minsk. (Genetic after-effects of radiation do not even get into the Appendix.) And then the world settles down to democracy. Nine end pages out of 360 are on 'The Beginning of the Future'. But, after survival, what? Silence. We might ask: was all this trouble really necessary?

This is an ostensibly blatant write-up in favour of an expanded NATO, *here and now*. It is a cynical invitation to despair. It is a subtle piece of *War* propaganda that follows the smooth Goebbels technique of inevitable destiny. For it all looks so easy. Hackett sets up row after row of WAPO aunt-sallies, so that he can knock them down like ninepins. He changes the 'unlikely' into the 'inevitable' with unerring skill. How can we contradict so honourable a gentleman?

1985 is a good date to choose, because by then the hackneyed Orwellian legend '1984' – another Utopia-in-reverse nightmare (written in 1949) – will have run out of steam and need revving up. But it is all very strange that, since the carefully limited 'nuclear exchange' – Birmingham *v.* Minsk – could be so successfully manipulated ahead of time (through the Hot Line?) with only a couple of million charred and shrivelled corpses left behind, no one had even thought of arranging to stop the 'exchange' *before* it began! If Hot Line wars can nowadays be so efficiently stage-managed by the prescient general staff, why cannot their superb services be enlisted in the preventative cooling process *instead*?

One does not have to be a dyed-in-the-wool communist to see that to launch a Hitlerian *blitzkrieg* in central Europe would be an act of blind idiocy for the Soviet military hierarchy, quite apart from reprisals the West would immediately take. The Kremlin might consist of a lot of inhuman and amoral men, but it is surely not a ship of fools intent on their own and their country's suicide.

The case against this type of wish-fulfilment war game can be condensed into three short, blunt sentences:

(1) Nobody *wants* it – neither Easterners nor Westerners, except a few crackpots;

(2) The best minds in the US and USSR are working against military confrontations at a thousand growing points of agree-

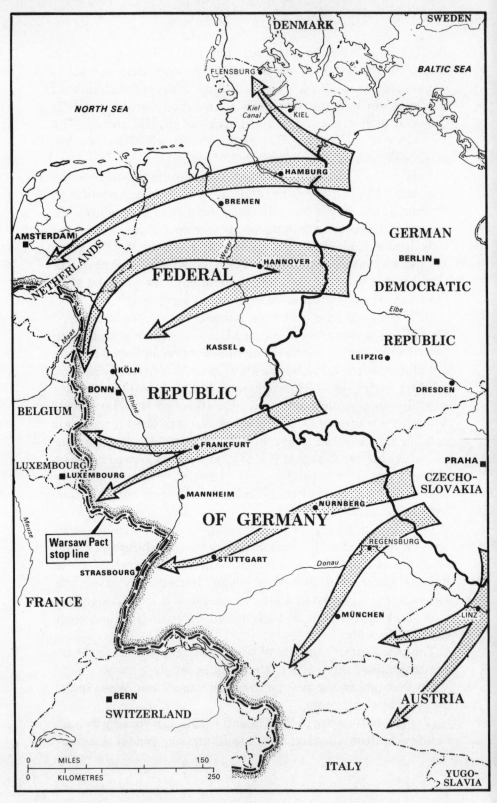

Map 2   The Soviet Plan to attack Western Europe in General Hackett's *Third World War, August 1985*

ment and co-operation, though both countries are plagued by their unrepentant hawks;

(3) For three decades a whole new system of planetary peace management – where US and USSR sit side by side at the UN – has been building up a structure of alternative options focused on common interests.

All of these compelling moves are conveniently omitted from the Hackett game, simply because, if they were included, his stacked deck would collapse.

To sum up. We cannot re-fight World War II, even with its allies switched, with World War III weapons. Nonetheless, the plan does warn us what the generals are up to. As the book gets around it will be an eye-opener for many ordinary citizens on how sinister a web of illusions NATO advance thinkers – General Hackett is one – have spun around them while they slept. Translated into Russian, it is bound to put them wise what to *avoid*, if taken seriously at all. But no doubt Soviet comic books will seize on it first. Russian humour always needs a grave subject to work on, as when Nikita Khrushchev jokingly replied to a journalist's question about America's superior nuclear capacity: 'Yes, I know what Kennedy claims, and he's quite right. But I'm not complaining . . . We're satisfied to be able to finish off the United States first time round. Once is quite enough. What good does it do to annihilate a country twice? We're not a bloodthirsty people.'

A recipient of the 1959 Nobel Peace Prize and a member of the British delegation to the UN Special Session on Disarmament in 1978, Lord Noel-Baker stands at the opposite end of the spectrum of international luminaries. He took his first stance for peace more than half a century ago as a conscientious objector to World War I. Serving instead in a wartime ambulance corps, he spent some time 'in my dugout', he recalls, writing an essay for a competition on ideas for forming a League of Nations. Philip Noel-Baker went on to serve in the British delegation to the League's Disarmament Conferences in 1932–34, an effort which he says 'very nearly succeeded'. He still thinks that there might be peace *now*, if we got rid of the warmongers. When Lord Noel-Baker speaks on the arms race, there is no doubting the spirit and sharpness of a man who has devoted the better part of his 90 years to the cause of world disarmament: 'It's all the fault of those bloody hawks. If we could get rid of them, and get people to realize the dangers of a nuclear war, we would have a beautiful world.'

It is not clear whether General Hackett had at any time consulted the weighty signatories of the UN experts' report (cited above), who take quite a different view of what would happen if so-called 'tactical' weapons were let loose over European cities. They say:

In certain quarters it is still military doctrine that any disparity in the conventional strength of opposing forces could be redressed by using nuclear weapons in the zone of battle. Carefully conducted and dispassionate theoretical studies of the use of nuclear weapons in field warfare, including analyses of an extensive series of 'war games' relating to the European theatre, have led to the clear conclusion that this military doctrine could lead to the use of hundreds, and not of tens, of so-called tactical nuclear weapons in the battlefields ... It can be firmly stated that, were nuclear weapons to be used in this way, they could lead to the devastation of the whole battle zone.

Military planners have no past experience on which to call for any guide as to how military operations could proceed in circumstances such as these. When such levels of physical destruction are reached, one might well ask what would determine the course of a nuclear battle? Would it be the number of enemy casualties? Would it be the violent psychological reaction, fear and terror, to the horror of widespread instantaneous destruction? Would the chaos immediately bring all military operations to a halt?

Perhaps General Hackett's next book will answer these questions. Meanwhile, the aforementioned experts stress: 'The same would apply to larger so-called "clean" weapons used in a strategic role. In this case there would in addition be considerable induced radio-activity caused by the capture of neutrons in atmospheric nitrogen, thus producing very long-lived radioactive carbon-14. So far as long-range and long-term fall-out is concerned, this radio-active hazard from so-called "clean" weapons is comparable in importance to that from less "clean" weapons.' (As a matter of fact, we might add, all nuclear weapons are unclean, and the answer is *DON'T*!)

The ominous fall-out of the Hackett plan is already reaching grotesque proportions. As war talk spreads, local authorities in England are being swamped by householders begging to know how to 'protect' themselves. Advice on how best to survive a nuclear attack has been published by a British organization called Civil Aid. Mr Robin Meads, vice-chairman of Civil Aid, told a press conference that after a nuclear attack hungry people would have to take what they could get: 'If you saw a frog running about, you would have to wash it to get rid of active dust, cook it and eat it.' His pamphlet admits that food for 14 days, batteries, candles and other essentials are not available in sufficient quantities for a last-minute rush by the whole British population. 'So reasonable steps must be taken in advance. Coal, coke, wood and fir-cones will produce heat, but many houses have no fireplaces, and so paraffin, methylated spirits and bottled gas seem the only substitute for normal electricity or piped gas.' The pamphlet wisely counsels: 'A hay-box used for slow cooking will save a large proportion of heat.' This advice is remarkably similar to the Government's own *Protect and Survive* booklet; but how to preserve that hay-box in 2,000 degrees of nuclear heat is omitted from both.

At bottom, it is really very sad that General Hackett's doctrines should have led him into so blind an alley. For he is undoubtedly an honest and a good man. His brilliant career, in war and peace, has always earned the highest commendation of his fellows, civil and military. It is not on those grounds that his book is to be deplored as an insult to commonsense and a grave assault on the human spirit.

Professor Gilbert Murray, Greek scholar and humanist, and for many years the Chairman of the League of Nations Union in pre-war Britain, used to say solemnly to us neophytes who worked with him, that war was not caused by bad men. It was a conflict between good men and good men, because only good men could defend its horrors and imbecilities; they did so in the name of some ideal beyond themselves. No one can deny the sacrifice and self-abnegation that war has brought to millions and millions of individuals – a sacrifice and self-abnegation that other men, smaller men, have exploited and corrupted for lesser ends. So war has been given, because of these higher ideals, a glamour and social status that later evaluations have proved to be exaggerated and spurious, as well as disastrous for mankind. Modern anthropologists include it among cultural acquisitions that are neither necessary nor permanent. War is now obsolete.

However tolerable for past centuries, the depersonalization of modern war, with its endless range of death techniques and mutilation machines, has taken the goodness out of war. We should have learnt this long ago. Even an old warrior like Winston Churchill, in *My Early Life*, wrote:

War, which used to be cruel and magnificent, has now become cruel and squalid . . . Instead of a small number of well-trained professionals championing their country's cause with ancient weapons and a beautiful intricacy of archaic manoeuvre, sustained at every moment by the applause of their nation, we now have entire populations, including even women and children, pitted against one another in brutish mutual extermination, and only a set of blear-eyed clerks left to add up the butcher's bill. From the moment Democracy was admitted to, or rather forced itself upon the battlefield, War has ceased to be a gentleman's game. To Hell with it!

It is not 'democracy' that has changed the battlefield from a gentleman's game to a genocidal charnel house. It is modern military technology that has made nonsense of any democracy 'on the battlefield'. Nuclear warheads are not the language of gentlemen, but the idiom of murderers – megamurderers.

The *coup-de-grâce* against Hackett's B *v.* M War Game (Birmingham *v.* Minsk) was delivered by the late Earl Mountbatten in a speech at Strasbourg on 11 May 1979:

Next month I enter my eightieth year. I am one of the few survivors of the First World War who rose to high command in the Second and I know how impossible it is to pursue military operations in accordance with fixed plans and agreements . . . When I was Chief of the British Defence Staff I made my views known. I have heard the arguments against this view, but I have never found them convincing. So I repeat in all sincerity as a military man that I can see no use for any nuclear weapons which would not end in escalation, with consequences that no-one can conceive.

(2) Would a continental war really work?

The following capsule arguments by the Center for Defense Information (Washington DC) are backed up by defence analysts all round the globe:

The possibility of a conventional non-nuclear war in Europe is slim.

Neither the US nor USSR will go to war for less than national survival and each will use its complete arsenal to win once war has started.

Any military conflict in Europe between East and West forces would quickly escalate to nuclear weapons.

- The neutron weapon is irrelevant to the defence of Western Europe. NATO has sufficient tactical nuclear weapons to deter or to fight a war if needed.

The Warsaw Pact cannot conduct a surprise attack against NATO forces without prior warning.

NATO military efforts should be directed at *avoiding* war in Europe rather than fighting a war in Europe.

For over thirty years (i.e. since NATO began) the USA has sought to 'protect' Europe from the Russians. This is sometimes referred to by MPs and press correspondents as the 'nuclear umbrella'! For those same thirty years Russia has stayed put behind the same buffer states that she consolidated as her agreed 'defence' zone at the end of World War II, and actually confirmed in the Helsinki agreements in 1975.

But the hawks are never satisfied. Somehow, something extra has always been needed by the Pentagon planners to tilt the alleged balance their way.

Seven thousand or more so-called 'tactical' nukes – i.e. 7,000 super-Hiroshimas – still don't do the trick, even though the Russians have fewer of them. Something more reassuring must therefore be put on the ground level. So the neutron weapon suddenly sprang in 1978 into the Western headlines and opened a Pandora's Box of agonizing argument. Fortunately, public opinion – at last – had something to say. For one thing, the neutron case rested on two very doubtful assumptions, namely: (1) that a war started in Europe could remain conventional; and (2) that nuclear war with tactical nuclear weapons could be limited to Europe.

That is the Hackett line. But neither proposition makes sense. NATO and WAPO would fight a conventional war only as long as each could foresee itself winning. But, if neither could expect to win such a war quickly – a reasonable assumption – the losing side would have to resort to nuclear weapons in desperation. US Secretary of Defense Harold Brown has told the House Armed Services Committee: 'Any Soviet planner must consider that a successful Soviet massive conventional attack would trigger first tactical, then strategic nuclear weapons used against them.' This is the 'flexible response' doctrine, supported by the compliant British defence establishment.

It is irrelevant how clean or dirty are the tactical nuclear weapons. The essential question is how any responsible Soviet leader would *respond* to the NATO employment of even one such weapon. This is the Birmingham *versus* Minsk gambit. But a noted Soviet military writer, Marshal Sokolovskii, has stated: 'Once the military movements on land and sea have *started* they are no longer subject to the desires and plans of diplomacy, but rather to their own laws.'

Because of the fallacious 'balance' doctrine that has dominated every arms race, once war begins the momentum of military operations and the imperatives of survival and victory must take over. Political control will cease to exist. An enemy's battle intentions are always uncertain. Field commanders, unable to communicate quickly with their political leaders, will have recalled Montgomery's advice. The use of tactical nuclear weapons, after the first decision had been made, would be delegated to hard-pressed combat commanders fighting for their existence.

The conditions initiating a nuclear war, however 'limited' its initial intentions, could not be later controlled by an act of will. This is because the political will would itself *be lacking in the first place to prevent the war*. The uncertainty and fear surrounding what defence ministers and newspaper columnists glibly call

	NATO		Warsaw Pact	
	delivery systems	nuclear weapons	delivery systems	nuclear systems
Nuclear land mines	—	300	—	—
Heavy artillery	900	3,000	—	—
Surface-to-surface missiles	1,000	1,000	1,000	1,000
Surface-to-air missiles	500	500	—	—
Tactical aircraft	2,000	3,900	2,350	2,500
Total	4,400	8,700	3,350	3,500

Table 4   Tactical nuclear weapons and delivery systems currently deployed in Europe (estimates rounded).
Source: Center for Defense Information estimate

a 'nuclear exchange' could only result in the nuclear disaster that both US and Soviet Union political leadership have sought to avoid.

It is important to get things into stark perspective. NATO's original strategy did not begin with all these off-beat imponderables. The US *started* the race with the monopoly of the A-bomb and, then, the H-bomb. They relied on them for 'national defence', not their allies. This was long before the Russians began to catch up with them. It was Secretary of State John Foster Dulles who, with evangelistic fervour, invented the era of 'massive retaliation'. This relied on the dominant *threat* of US strategic bombers and nuclear retaliation to deter any threats to West European security. The umbrella fantasy followed.

However, the Russians were not concerned with American defence. But with Russian defence. So, as the Moscow planners strengthened *their* nuclear capability, 'massive retaliation' lost its relevance as a deterrent. Mutual retaliation would guarantee a nuclear war which no one would win. Thus, after prolonged debate in NATO councils, the Alliance adopted in December

1967 the more costly strategy of 'flexible response', which theoretically provided *multiple* war-fighting options, if conflict did begin.*

This new flexible response strategy assumed that the US and its European allies could *contain* a Soviet attack initially without nuclear weapons, but it also assumed that nuclear weapons would be used if we could not stop 'Soviet aggression'. The irrelevance of all this to the Afghanistan situation is now evident. The United States has even proposed that, with increasing numbers of non-nuclear forces, there would be 'no need' to use nuclear weapons at all in Europe. The very flexibility of this flexible response has naturally diminished the credibility of its deterrent objective. Yet it has succeeded in nurturing a continuing debate within the Alliance, which continues to undermine NATO's unity. This became obvious at the end of 1979 when the Netherlands Government – and public opinion – refused to play with the 572 Pentagon missiles. The revolt continues.

When the US Senate recently approved a $3.8 billion military construction bill, it refused to authorize any of the combat-construction projects for Europe, as sought by the Carter administration. Senator John Stennis, chairman of the Armed Services Committee, pointed out that much of the $375 million in combat-related 'construction requested for NATO is an Alliance responsibility that should not be unilaterally funded by the United States'. So the divided Allies were being pressured to dig deeper into their own pockets, to pay for the American arms imports. To protect whom? Yet one thing that the NATO strategy of flexible response has done is to intensify the conventional arms build-up on *both* sides. So back to Square One.

The bad joke of all this nuclear shadow-boxing is that the Soviet Union itself, as far as we know, has never accepted the concept of conventional war in Europe. The Soviet Union continues to reject the idea that a major war in Europe could remain non-nuclear. They have at least commonsense on their side. In so far as they consider nuclear warfare inevitable in such a war, can they not be expected to employ nuclear weapons at the outset – rather than leave the choice to NATO?

*The author has analysed the history of NATO and its failings in his book *The End of an Illusion*, Allen and Unwin, 1968

Ground Forces	
Main battle tanks	886
Other armoured vehicles	4,014
Artillery pieces	453
Anti-tank weapon systems	22,736
Naval Forces	
Destroyers/escorts	21
Attack submarines	9
Fast patrol boats	29
Minelayers/minesweepers	19
Air Forces/Air Defence	
Combat aircraft	331
Helicopters	277
Anti-aircraft guided missile systems	745
Anti-aircraft guns	997

Table 5   New weapons added by European NATO Forces, 1976–78 (excluding increases in US weapons positioned in Europe).
Source: US Department of Defense

Even a US deputy secretary of defence, Mr Morton Halperin, has said: 'The NATO doctrine is to fight with conventional arms until we are losing, then to fight with nuclear tacticals until we are losing, and then to blow up the world.'

One Soviet military commentator has actually stated: 'It has been proved that under present-day conditions local or limited wars would be nothing but the prelude to a general missile-nuclear war.' Although the Soviet Union has now placed renewed emphasis on its conventional forces, as a response to the recent change in NATO's own emphasis on conventional forces, Soviet leaders continue to recognize that nuclear weapons would definitely be used in a major war (somehow) confined to Europe. Soviet Marshal Sokolovskii announced bluntly: 'The basic means for armed combat in land theatres in a future world war will be the nuclear weapons.' This is precisely the late Earl Mountbatten's conviction.

Nonetheless, despite the likelihood of any WAPO aggression quickly escalating into a full-scale nuclear conflict, NATO has been encouraging the costly military build-up on both sides, thus increasing the tension that could precipitate such a war. In

1977 the US spent $46 billion – over 40 per cent of its military budget – for the 'defence' of Europe. The Allies contributed upwards of $60 billion. As stated above, because of the worsening economic crisis in the US and the 'fall' of the dollar, Congressmen in 1978 and 1979 were pleading with NATO allies to pay more for America's gift-horses. Hence, the cost of the 572 'upgraded' nuclears in the 1980s now falls on the Europeans. Since its inception 32 years ago, NATO has continually strengthened its conventional forces. Yet for these 32 years its military leaders have maintained that these forces were still 'not adequate'. Adequate for what? Does *anybody* know?

In late 1978 a veritable barrage of propaganda burst out in press and political speeches on 'the Russian threat'. This pushed the totals higher still. As Tennyson wrote: 'Is there any peace in ever climbing up the ever climbing wave?' Suddenly, however, from out of the blue in early 1980, the 'threat' shifted to Afghanistan (which shares a thousand kilometres of frontier with the USSR). The imminent invasion of Europe miraculously dropped out of the editorials. The causes of World War III had shifted to a side street in Teheran.

There is a sullen perception of less security today than when NATO initiated its military build-up in 1949 – always well ahead of WAPO (1955). As long as the myth of NATO's failure to outmatch Soviet improvements persists, US policy-makers and their compliant UK camp-followers, will push and push for more and more. This is the pseudo-logic, the imbecile momentum of the arms race: filling up the bottomless pit.

Meanwhile, Secretary of Defense Harold Brown has been constantly enhancing the *readiness* of US home forces to provide *rapid reinforcement* to NATO. Combat units in Europe and selected divisions in the US are manned at 100 per cent to improve *combat readiness*, he has declared. (This was before the Afghanistan defection.) Stocks of replacement weapons and ammunition in Europe are now at their highest levels in the history of the Alliance.

Yet there is still not enough to go around. For, with the Iranian revolution in 1979, the next stage was to plan mobile units of 100,000 men destined for the Gulf region and to play down Europe. Some Americans, however, have recognized that the Gulf states might have different political and military needs from the US. What is good for General Motors is not always good for OPEC. The 'security' framework proposed by President Carter would comprise separate relations with each country in the region, not a uniform alliance. (CENTO, the ugly sister of NATO in the Middle East, had long ago faded away like a bad dream.)

However, in January 1980, Kuwait's Foreign Minister Sabah al-Ahmed called on the Arab world to devise a strategy confronting *both* Washington and Moscow. He said that the Israeli occupation of the West Bank was backed by the United States and was 'no less serious' than the Soviet intervention in Afghanistan. The great powers were gambling at the expense of small countries around the Gulf. Nor was he alone. The United Arab Emirates complained that the United States was using the Soviet action in Afghanistan as an excuse to expand its military presence in the Gulf. So what next? Will our World War III planners amend the NATO treaty so as to stretch the American umbrella now as far as Pakistan?

Reverting to Europe, NATO spending is higher today than at any time in the past decade. In 1971–1976, NATO allies in Europe showed a real increase of 11 per cent in military spending. Together, the US and its NATO allies spent over a 100 *billion* dollars in 1977 for military forces in Europe alone. Now the United States has insisted on an arms budget expansion of at least three per cent annual 'real growth', that is, three per cent over and above inflation. But are we getting our money's worth? This is not merely climbing up the ever-climbing wave, it is sending a financial helicopter above it. And we know how unpredictable helicopters are!

Admiral Gene R. La Rocque, US Navy (Ret.), redoubtable Director of the Center for Defense Information in Washington, states that 'conventional war of any duration would be virtually impossible in Europe today'. The question has been asked, however: 'Could the Soviets penetrate NATO defences quickly and achieve their objectives before Allied decisions have been made to use nuclear weapons in their defence?' He replies that the success of such a Soviet *blitzkrieg* would depend on two factors: (1) their ability to carry out a surprise attack and, then, (2) quickly penetrate NATO defences, seizing key objectives in Western Europe.

He might also have answered the primary question: *Why* did they want to do this? But he cites General Michael Davison, former Commander of the US Army in Europe: 'The Warsaw Pact commanders are sure to realize that the NATO Central Army Group defense deployment is capable of inflicting significant damage on their forces should they attack. This uncertainty of the prospects for a quick and easy advance to the NATO heartland is reinforced with equal uncertainty as to whether and when we might resort to nuclear weapons.' General Hackett would seem to have missed this point.

Against the 'uncertainty' (i.e. military guesswork) of these backroom strategists, one has to set the patent megalomania of Washington's political bosses, who were so thrown off course by the Iranian challenge. In an address to the International Platform Association in Washington on 2 August 1979, Mr Zbigniew Brzezinski, President Carter's hawkish adviser for national security, lumped together the Middle and the Far East as being on a par with Western Europe:

> The American military power must be in a position to protect our essential interests abroad, including the three vital strategic zones beyond our Hemisphere: Western Europe, the Near and the Far East. This means we must assure that we have the reach and the means to project our power where it is needed, and to do so in the appropriate form and level of intensity. In this task we consult [*sic*] our allies and friends in every realm, co-operate with them and react on their wishes. *But we remain the leader and must bear the burdens of that role*. [Our italics].

Much has been written about the Soviet capability for a 'massive surprise attack' against Western Europe, yet that possibility is more conjecture than fact. But endless repetition transforms conjecture into reality. Russian intentions in the Gulf areas are even more vague and 'uncertain'. Historically, this kind of attack has rarely occurred. Periods of festering crisis have preceded all major conflicts in the past century. Nations may have remained unprepared, but not because there were no advance indications or warnings. Admiral Sir Peter Hill-Nortom has called such a surprise attack scenario 'nonsense'. General Alexander Haig, a NATO hawk, has added: 'The NATO agreed-on

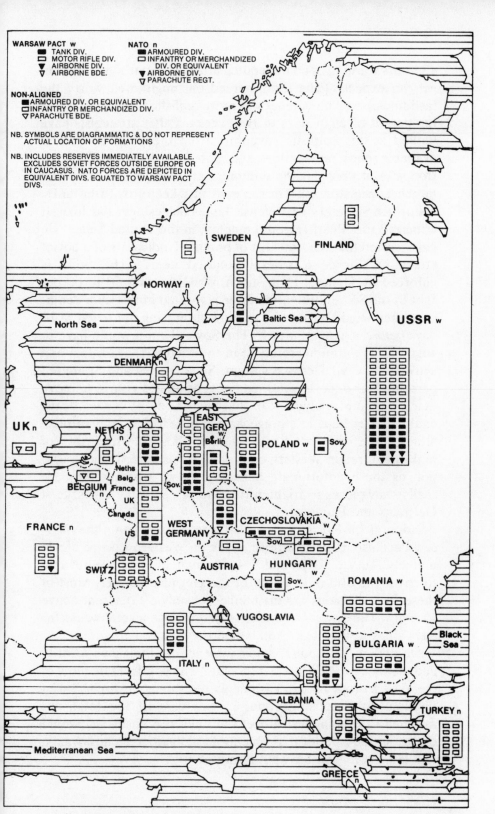

Map 3   NATO/Warsaw Pact Forces in Europe

*Greece's membership of NATO is in the balance.

48 hours warning of an impending attack is the absolute bottom we can expect.' (The term 'agreed-on' might well worry the fastidious.) And he noted it was more realistic to expect a warning period of eight days to two weeks. Other strategists have looked at this fantastic adventure from the point of view of available roads, railway lines, and canteens to feed the advancing troops; and they put the minimum at 20 days. An army still marches on its stomach. The canteens must keep up with the tanks.

Former Secretary of Defense James Schlesinger has himself criticized the 'Pearl Harbor complex' in the United States. He has asserted that the 'total list of potential indicators of a Soviet attack in Europe is several hundred items'. This point is enforced by General Haig, again, who says that 50 to 60 per cent of the Soviet submarine force is located in the Kola Peninsula; they would have to be put to sea, moving out seven to 14 days *before* a general attack. The Soviet Union would have to augment its outnumbered fleet in the Mediterranean, too, and activate its Civil Defence system. Soviet tanks and armoured personnel carriers show no readiness of their divisions to move quickly. Some analysts fear that two-thirds of Soviet heavy equipment is kept in storage and is unready for the surprise attack. One does not know whether those massive rows of tanks, featured in Western editorials, are as defective in operation as those unfortunate helicopters – or whether they are really showpieces to frighten (in case of need) the Poles, East Germans and Rumanians.

Admiral La Rocque states that weaknesses within the Warsaw Pact also make a surprise attack on Western Europe highly unlikely. The 26 Soviet and East German divisions are not able to cover the 300-mile length of the German frontier. Most of these Pact divisions are maintained at only 50 per cent active strength. The Soviets would be forced to wait several weeks for *their* allies to mobilize. And would they?

Do any of these buffer states *want* to lose their own security and march across Europe? If so, *why*? The political reliability of the East European states is deeply questionable. Eight Soviet divisions in Eastern Europe, 25 per cent of the total, are assigned to keeping watch over their allies. A costly war would create serious political problems in Poland, Czechoslovakia, and Hungary. And for what purpose?

How much cold-war brainwashing does it need to take the 'Russian threat' seriously? We have taken time to analyse this Western-made spectre because of the millions of reams of newsprint that have been devoted throughout the 1960s and 1970s to feed NATO's egotism and expanding budgets.

This analysis does not answer every doubting Thomas, but it does show that the Soviet juggernaut is more myth than reality. NATO planners discount the real problems facing even the élite Soviet divisions. As US General Davison has argued: 'the (Warsaw) Pact forces are not ten feet tall. They have some major disadvantages which permit us to place them in a more realistic perspective.' This is not the same story (for reasons we need not examine) of Soviet tanks and planes moving in January 1980 smoothly across their own southern border and finding a 'WELCOME' message already displayed at the Kabul airport by the pro-communist Afghanistan Government. There is a legal aphorism: 'Analogy is no argument'. But the public is fed analogies all the time. A year or more will pass before the miscalculations and stupidities of the Afghan invasion are seen in their historical and geographical perspective. In the meantime, the damage will have been done, all round.

Yet, since the comparison has been often made concerning the invasion of communist Czechoslovakia in 1968, thousands of vehicles and equipment had to be requisitioned from farms and factories in the Soviet Union. Soviet field armies must also operate in Europe within 80 to 90 miles of their own railheads; but their railheads are vulnerable to air attack and are more difficult to repair than roads. The ability of Soviet forces to conduct even the most limited operations would depend on the adequacy of vehicle maintenance. But need we go on to stress the obvious? And all this happened – however deplorable – *within* the Warsaw Pact area twelve years ago, while NATO looked on helplessly and the United States forces were enmeshed in the jungles of Vietnam.

Meanwhile, the '48 hours' notice' syndrome of a Russian attack has been taken seriously by the British Government and a European mock war has been designed on the *assumption* that an enemy offensive has been launched against the West. Since this exercise, called Crusader 80, had been in planning for over a year and is described by Whitehall sources as the most com-

91

prehensive war game for many years, it can hardly have been the result of the Afghanistan crisis. But as it had not taken place at the time this book was written, further comment would be superfluous; some estimate of its cost and scope, however, can be gathered from the following brief summary from *The Times* Defence Correspondent (21 March 80): '£8.5m military exercise, the biggest of its kind since the Second World War, will be held in Britain and West Germany in September. About 30,000 troops, including nearly 20,000 part-timers from the Territorial Army, will be drafted across the Channel to reinforce the British Army of the Rhine.'

Admiral La Rocque proposes, instead of NATO's shadow-boxing, a 'War Avoidance' campaign. His proposals, as a military man, strike an air of commonsense. They are extremely important and are worth setting down in his own terms:

> The adoption of a 'war avoidance' strategy would not mean that conventional forces no longer have an important role to play. In Europe, however, the existence of nuclear weapons in large numbers on both sides has made conventional forces less important than they were in the past two world wars . . . The US must rid itself of the presumptuous delusion that only the presence of large American ground forces in Europe stands in the way of aggression and political domination of the continent by the Soviet Union. Europe is not ours to lose. The Europeans have historically fought in their own defense and have no intention of giving up their independence to anyone – particularly not to the Soviet Union.

He insists that a 'war avoidance' strategy would face positively what is in fact the situation in Europe today. To continue the self-delusion that a war in Europe would *not* quickly escalate into a nuclear war or to downplay the catastrophic dangers of such a war is a far more hazardous alternative: 'European NATO's interests and capabilities must be tightly folded into the balanced strategic relationship between the US and the Soviet Union, rather than considered separately as under our present "conventional war posture".' Such a clear commitment would not lack credibility, the Admiral states: 'This policy may be more appropriate today than ever before. Our role of world

92

policeman has diminished and a perceived commitment to Europe would be more credible precisely because it is coldly rational and selective.'

His point is that by eliminating the ambivalence of the current US posture and emphasizing the commitment to furnishing the nuclear shield for Europe, a 'war avoidance' strategy would both discourage acceptance of the short-war *blitzkrieg* concept and the ever-present urge to increase conventional weapons and forces on both sides.

At last, we are beginning to see the light at the end of the tunnel – *war avoidance*! Is there a better place to stop the arms race? Security will grow as we put the arms race into reverse. That is the crucial turning point for decency and humanity. But have the US and the UK Governments set up study groups of disarmament experts and peace researchers working on war avoidance? If not, why not? Why not Royal Commissions and Congressional Committees on War Avoidance? Why not eight thousand million pounds for war avoidance? Who is stopping us – the Russians or ourselves?

(3) Who wants a Blitzkrieg anyway?

Something the Western military hawks forget or never knew (since they were probably not then born) is that Lenin's Russia came near to complete extinction from 1918 to 1922. The Bolsheviks were fighting not only the 'whites', but the *six invading armies* of the West. The young half-baked Republic was attacked from four seas – the White Sea, Baltic Sea, Black Sea and Caspian Sea; from north and south, east and west. British tommies and American doughboys, Poles and Czechs, Finns and Germans, pressed in on Moscow and Leningrad from all directions. They were thrown back. The October 1917 Revolution had won. Not all revolutions are pretty things to outsiders, but they mean a great deal to the people who suffered and died to bring them about.

'Never again!' The common people of the Soviet Union have echoed this cry for 60 years. You can't expect them to change that cry, now surrounded by a worldwide line-up of 'capitalist' weaponry and NATO strategy.

Yet it nearly did 'happen again'. In 1941 Hitler's tanks suddenly swept through from devastated Poland. They ravaged Russia right up to the very suburbs, again, of Moscow and Leningrad, leaving behind them a third of Mother Russia gutted and blackened – with twenty million Soviet citizens dead from shells, bombs, or starvation. These are living facts. No Russian today forgets them.

The story of Russia's bloody victory and incredible sacrifices and final recovery against Nazi Germany should be too well known to need repeating. But 'never again!' swells louder today throughout the land. It doesn't need Kremlin propaganda to stimulate it. Yet it is not loud enough for the war-hawks of the West to hear. On the contrary, the same (illegally) over-armed and divided Germany – or, at least, two-thirds of it in the West – is now equipped with countless missile sites mathematically aimed to destroy all of Russia's major cities. In the 1980s, as we have seen, West Germany will receive *most* of the 572 new warheads from Washington. And our politicians are telling us: 'This gives *us* security.'

Most of the Soviet people are convinced that their preoccupation with defence is well founded. The compulsion to provide security at any cost has nearly always overridden everything else. President John F. Kennedy said on 10 June, 1963:

No nation in the history of battle ever suffered more than the Soviet Union suffered in the course of the Second World War. At least 20 million lost their lives. Countless millions of homes and farms were burned or sacked. A third of the nation's territory, including nearly two thirds of its industrial base, was turned into a wasteland – a loss equivalent to the devastation of this country east of Chicago.

The Russian people in the 20th century have suffered the horror of war on a scale that perhaps no other country has experienced. What Soviet leaders believe to be adequate defence forces will be likely to differ from what others think.

Viewed through Soviet eyes and in historical context, much of their military effort is aimed at overcoming vulnerabilities and matching American, NATO, as well as Chinese capabilities. Soviet fears of military dangers can be greater than those of Americans. Thus:

The Russian obsession with national defense has deep historical roots and permeates Soviet society. It creates dangers of over-reaction to past weaknesses and could cause them to go beyond the basic requirements of defense. (Admiral Gene R. La Rocque).

How would *you* look at all this, if you were on the other side of the missile curtain – a normal average Soviet citizen? Forget about communism, but would you – as a Russian – want to throw away 35 years of co-existence by a sudden massive and suicidal thrust into Western Europe? If so, where would you be *going*? (No one ever tells us that.) To Portugal or Spain or the mid-Atlantic? Where would such a crash programme *finish*? What would happen afterwards?

The Soviet Union is a country whose history has instilled in its national spirit an understandable deep-seated *fear* of foreign threats. Within one generation, as shown above, Russian territory has been occupied by foreign military forces for three extended periods. Neither Britain nor the USA knows this experience. Efforts to deal with contemporary issues today are merged with the memories of the carnage and appalling destruction of World War II. Unlike the US self-induced pathological fear of 'communism', these are facts, as they appear to the normal Soviet citizen. The persistence of the 'siege' mentality, accentuated nowadays by the cold war, and the deep-rooted nationalism of many Russians, exerts a powerful influence on all Soviet policy. Dissidents face this apprehension in the Soviet courts. The Kremlin can't give an inch. Most of the Soviet people are convinced that their preoccupation with defence is well-founded. The compulsion to provide security at any cost has nearly always overridden everything else. A workable disarmament plan is the best gift the West can give to the *people* of Russia.

Perhaps the greatest contrast between American and Soviet military matters is in the degree of secretiveness that surrounds Soviet military affairs. This policy of secrecy in military matters dates far back into Russian history. In the 20th century it has been reinforced by the bitter experiences of World Wars I and II. Technical information on military forces is not freely available, not even to the military. Officials in the Soviet Foreign Ministry have little or no access to data on Soviet military force levels. They probably know more about Western military developments than about their own. Excessive military secrecy stimulates suspicion and mistrust – and not only in Russia! This was encapsulated in an amusing remark by US Deputy Defense Secretary Roswell Gilpatric back in 1962: 'The Soviets are forced to work hard to match efforts that they *know* we are making to match efforts that we *think* they are making!'

How mad can communists be? Or are we not all just as mad? Where *are* the Soviet plans and time-tables for defending 'the Motherland' by launching a Hackett-type mutual destruction on the West – except in terms of territorial self-defence? The Soviet Union itself announces no such plan either to its own people (who obviously must be got ready for it) or to the world at large. All is conjecture.

Quite the reverse. All Soviet propaganda is focused time and time again on all-round cuts in armed forces and destruction of nuclear stock-piles. The 250,000,000 Soviet citizens would have to make a quick change of view to accept such a 48-hour *initiative*, however it was dressed up by the Kremlin. But it all falls on deaf ears in the West. The Russians are coming! The race must go on to beat them.

In October 1979 Brezhnev, in a surprise speech, offered as a *starter* to withdraw 1,000 tanks and 20,000 troops. Was this (genuine or not) taken in the West as a 'war avoidance' gesture? Every type of cold-war dialectic filled the editorial columns as to Brezhnev's motives and why the 572 upgraded warheads were the only valid form of Western response.

The cold-war columnists and politicos did not bother to set this latest effort to implement 'détente' within the context of Soviet disarmament policy ever since (not to go back further) Nikita Khrushchev took over from Stalin in 1955 and proposed in July that year to dissolve both NATO and the newly formed Warsaw Treaty in favour of an *all-European system of security* to include all states. During the negotiations for a partial nuclear test-ban treaty in 1963 *(see Appendix (A))* Krushchev tried again to get a non-aggression treaty between NATO and the 'Warsaw' nations. Since his ouster in 1965, the United Nations agendas have carried year by year Soviet proposals (even if some are phoney) to limit or halt the arms race, which the West automatically pigeonholes or side-steps. That is happening *now* in Geneva at the (barely reported) sessions of the new UN Disarmament Committee. Both Russia and China are there.

Are we in the West to believe that Kremlin leaders today are planning to destroy the fruits and stability (in their opinion) of 60 years of communist growth and consolidation by 'taking over Europe'? Can it be that the hard-line generals and political advisers and parrot-like news-media are on the wrong track, always turning the remotely 'possible' into the quite 'probable'? Are we being misled by our own bellifists into running the wrong war by the wrong people for the wrong reasons? Who wants a *blitzkrieg*, but the arms profiteers and a handful of military egos – they exist on both sides – who love to play war games for a living?

(4) Revving up the Cold War

It may be objected that the foregoing analysis puts too much blame on the United States and its policy-makers. There is a reason for this. Anyone who (like this author) has spent half an adult lifetime moving across the United States will know how tragically the cold-war mentality has blighted and corrupted both the Republic's domestic and foreign affairs ever since Harry Truman gave the signal to release the atomic bomb on Japan. The Hiroshima curse has lain like an evil omen on the conscience of the American people ever since. Underneath all the impassioned condemnation of the Soviets, millions of Americans ever since World War II have been unconsciously *expecting* the Russians to come and take them over!

This may sound absurd. And it was. But it is difficult for the average Britisher, brought up in a society where this obsessive fear does not exist, to bridge the psychological gap separating our two countries. Children were having regular drills in lying flat under their school-desks in California in the 1950s, as instructed by the local authorities. The noonday air-raid sirens whined their depressing warning regularly in New York and other cities year after year through the 1960s. Directions pointing to (quite inadequate) 'fall-out' and air-raid shelters still clutter up hotel staircases and school corridors. 'The Communist World Conspiracy' – no details were ever spelled out for the common folk – became an article of faith with countless after-dinner speakers and Jackson-type senators, urging arms increases, and with Ronald Reagan-type television stars, until the dominoes of the Vietnam War took its place.

Two months after his retirement in 1949, former Secretary of Defense James V. Forrestall had become so convinced of the communist 'threat' that when a fire-engine disturbed his sleep he ran out in his pyjamas, screaming that the Russians were coming. He committed suicide by jumping from the sixteenth floor. But before his mental illness was diagnosed, many Defense Department officials and the usual run of journalists accepted his anti-Soviet hallucinations for real, *whilst he was still in office*. The Russians are (rightly) blamed for their out-rageous practice of imprisoning dissidents in psychiatric hospitals. But how many statesmen, who are now seriously planning *real* war games, could pass a simple psychological test? We come back to this point later.

Once more, practically every newscast – whatever the subject – has been for a year or more loaded with the sickly spell of 'communist' misdoings. This was triggered in 1979 by the dis-covery of Soviet 'build-up', but no comparative figures ever appear in print to support this. The comparative charts in this book prove the opposite. Every American newspaper presents as American folk-lore the hysterical outpourings of dutiful editors and faithful columnists ferreting through every topic, no matter how remote – chess games, whale fishing, scholastic and athletic achievements – to prove to a susceptible audience that the Soviet Union *is* the 'enemy', an enemy to be out-manoeuvred and, somehow, eliminated. The timing of some of these scares is highly significant. As mentioned above, the 'news' of the escape of toxic chemicals in a mid-Siberian town came on the final day of the Geneva Conference convened to put a stop to chemical warfare.

We will pass over the obvious politicization of the Rosen-bergs' trials, the Hiss perjury persecution based on alleged treason (films hidden in a pumpkin!), and the purges of talented Hollywood scriptwriters, and even of great artists, during the McCarthy régime, so that neither Charlie Chaplin nor Paul Robeson could continue to live in America. This earlier period of persecution of liberal thought gave Richard Nixon to the Americans. The point is that a whole generation of adults has been brought up in an atmosphere of intimidation and hatred of communism. They are *now* Congressmen and leaders in public life, still clinging to the obsolete belief that terror weapons is the only language that the Russian people understand. The major speeches of the 1980 presidential election campaign were not about the health and welfare of America but the crimes of Russia. No one explains, in all these tirades, that Russia is not America, that the sad histories of the Warsaw Pact countries are so completely different from their own; and that the glorified self-image of the American Dream does not fit in at all with the pride and anguish of the Russian soul!

The recent emphasis by the United States President on human rights has actually worsened this already dangerous estrangement of two great countries. The ridiculous precedent of Senator Jackson's failing to swop American grain for Russian Jews was followed in the summer of 1978 by the massing of newspaper protests at a series of (to us) outrageous but (to the Russians) routine trials under Soviet internal law of leading Russian dissidents – a brave but very tiny segment of Soviet citizens.

But we can recall that this new onslaught was unexpectedly sandbagged by an unscripted interview in a French newspaper by Mr Andrew Young, then United States Ambassador at the United Nations. From out of the blue he said that he did not know what can happen to dissidents, because 'after all, in *our* prisons, too, there are hundreds, perhaps thousands of people whom I would describe as political prisoners. Ten years ago, I myself was standing trial in Atlanta for having organized a protest movement. Three years later, I was a Representative for Georgia. It is true that things do not change as quickly in the Soviet Union, *but they do change* all the same' (our italics).

When put on the official carpet for his truthfulness in telling what everybody knows, he explained that one *could not compare the American and Soviet systems*: 'I do not agree with this opposition between systems. Take the United States. Present-day American society has nothing in common with that before Franklin Roosevelt. In the thirties and forties, the trade union movement touched off a radical revolution in American life, without which we could certainly not produce today nine million cars a year. In the fifties, there was the revolution of civic and racial rights; today it is the women who intervene more and more in our economy. And this constant evolution is the rule everywhere.'

Then he astutely added: 'I think the present Soviet dissidents might well prove the salvation of the Soviet Union. They are a natural development of Soviet society, but its leaders have not yet understood it.' Ambassador Young added that he had no fears of a third world war breaking out. 'Our relations with the Soviet Union are much too good,' he said, 'and at all levels, *save publicly*.' Will this new America redeem the old?

Fortunately, sensible people recognize that, in many ways, Russia is one or more decades behind the West. This has always been true of Russian social history. It is surely time that Andy Young's insight was shared by all seekers after peace. It has long been the experience of this author that there are vast numbers of Andy Youngs in America, but few of them are able to make their way to the top in politics.

Dr Yuri Novikov is a Russian psychiatrist who worked for six years in the Serbsky Institute, where many well-known political dissidents have been incarcerated. A defector himself to London, he told *The Times* (17 July 1978) that he saw the misuse of psychiatry as a logical development of Russian history and the present system:

> For centuries Russians have been discouraged from pluralistic thinking. The methods of the KGB are the same as those of the nineteenth-century security services. Of course, strictly speaking, it is not *thinking* differently that is punished, but *acting* differently, which is why the KGB is always looking for concrete acts, such as currency offences, to pin on dissidents. But forcing people to act differently from the way they think leads to neurosis.

If the West considers itself superior in its attitude towards its own rebels and minorities, then that superiority could best be displayed on the *international* level in terms of the UN Charter's first requirement: 'To practise tolerance and live together in peace with one another as good neighbours.'

Another sensible American, former Secretary of State

Vance, said on 10 July 1978: 'The Strategic Arms Limitations Talks, which would lead to an agreement in that area, are of particular importance, as I have indicated on many, many occasions. They deal with the security of our nation, the security of the Soviet Union, and indeed, affect the peace of the world. Therefore they stand on their own two feet and have a special quality.' This is not the view of either the hard-core US Senate (who must eventually approve SALT II) or of the foremost of the UK journalistic hawks, Lord Chalfont, who expressly denigrates SALT and subjects it to his own theories about how the Soviet Union should handle human rights issues:

And to those who still insist that agreements with the Soviet Union should be pursued irrespective of that country's domestic political arrangements, it is important to put one simple question: what guarantee is there that a country which cynically ignores an international undertaking on human rights, signed by its own head of state, will have any greater regard for a treaty on nuclear weapons? (*The Times*, 17 July 1978).

These Western 'peace' dissidents will do all in their power to block any step, however slight and however reasonable, to establish good relations with the Soviet Union, particularly in the vital area of disarmament. What is their effect on the doves and hawks in the Kremlin? The hard-liners of the Kremlin's military complex must thank their lucky stars for the Jacksons and Chalfonts. As is well known, the US President's initiative to promote world human rights has been exploited in America as a further weapon against the Russians. The fallacy of the Chalfont double-think, quoted above, is that political dissidents, even under an oppressive authoritarian régime such as is Russia, would swell in numbers and significance if 'the security of the Soviet Union' became more assured along the lines that Cyrus Vance envisaged. There is a new call today to put international security before national weaponry.

Whatever views are entertained by citizens of the West about the internal politics of the Soviet Union, and the alleged 'build-up' of its conventional arms on the territory of Eastern Europe, it must be admitted that the United States has always led the nuclear race, which is the crux of the arms race. The US has consistently been the pacemaker and proud of the fact. It produced the *first* atomic bomb in 1945 (1949 for the Soviets); the *first* intercontinental bomber in 1948 (1954); the *first* nuclear-powered strategic submarines in 1960 (1968); the *first* MIRVed missiles in 1970 (1975). Now the *first* modern Cruise missile. The Russians later led the way with ICBMs and anti-ballistic missile systems, but the US quickly caught up. Every major advance by one side has been answered by the other side.

Why not be the *first to stop*? A reversal of the arms race can begin the same way. There is no mystery about unilateral disarmament. It is rearmament the other way round.

But there is another dimension, too. Richard J. Barnet, Founder of the Institute for Policy Studies, Washington, D.C., has rightly called 'deterrence' a massive hostage system. 'Most Americans are unwitting prisoners', and he concludes:

Security is fundamentally a spiritual and psychological problem. What we trust defines who we are as a nation. To develop the spiritual, psychological and economic resources for survival and growth, we will have to put our trust in something other than weapons stockpiles . . . The only way to stop the arms race is for both sides to communicate to each other a clear intention to stop.

IV
Holocaust as Big Business

The Duke of Kent opened in Aldershot in 1978 the British Army Equipment Exhibition, chief purpose of which was to boost the sales of arms to foreign countries, particularly the Third World. The Exhibition took place while the UN Special Disarmament Assembly was in session in New York. Two years later there was a repeat performance, but it was closed to the public. The *Observer* summed up the ambivalence of the British position:

> Britain's cross-purposes are well defined. In a carefully written speech at the UN two weeks ago, which was much praised by other delegates, Mr Callaghan spoke of Britain's central role in disarmament, and stressed that the suppliers of arms had a special responsibility to practise restraint. Yet only two weeks later teams of British salesmen are shouting their wares at an arms fair, to sell still more guns, tanks and ammunition to customers abroad. Where exactly does the special responsibility lie? . . . Among the images of the 1970s which may look most incomprehensible to our grandsons could be an arms fair under royal patronage, enthusiastically selling weapons to the Third World. (18 June 1978).

But vigorously protesting against the arms fair was the Campaign Against the Arms Trade – a federation of Churchmen, Liberals and pacifists – who had chosen 'Death Sales Week' as the slogan of their demonstration. As evidence of the growing split of public opinion in Britain over the death trade, a motion against the hypocrisy of the exhibition was also tabled in the House of Commons by six Labour MPs:

That this House notes the inconsistency of supporting the UN Special Session on Disarmament whilst simultaneously holding a Defence Sales Organization exhibition at Aldershot to boost the arms trade . . . and urges the Government to switch the 400 Defence Sales Organization staff to selling non-military British manufactures instead.

It does not follow, however, that this nation of shopkeepers is doing too well out of the arms business abroad. While the Ministry of Defence was equipping an 'arms sales' ship to visit four countries in 1978, the Royal Institute of International Affairs came out with a study dealing with the whole function of the British arms industry, which was employing 275,000 people on work worth some £3,000 million a year. *About a quarter of this is for export*.

The report ignores the moral question of exporting lethal weapons for profit, but does go into the extent to which arms sales have actually eased defence costs. It says that unless an overseas order can directly follow the completion of a domestic order, the cost of equipment to the British armed services will not be reduced. Moreover, such equipment from Royal Ordnance factories may not only fail to make a profit, but may even fail to contribute to the cost of fixed overheads. In short, British arms sales *cannot be justified on budgetary grounds*, but must be judged by the extent to which they sustain British technological capacity. But this, too, is limited because the bulk of British sales are in trainer planes, helicopters and patrol boats, rather than high-technology products such as advanced combat aircraft.

In any case, the Services dislike being turned into a sales promotion organization and expect their equipment to be designed to meet British requirements, rather than those of potential customers. In the case of the Shah of Iran's orders for a new mark of Chieftain tank, British servicemen saw another country getting equipment that would not be available to the

104

BAOR for at least five years. (It may shock a new generation of readers to know that Britain still has an Army on the Rhine, which will cost in 1980 £763,000,000.)

The build-up of arms in the developing countries, which have taken about 75 per cent of British arms exports, appears to have passed its peak. Several of these countries are starting to develop their own arms industries, so the future for such products may well be limited. The Chatham House report indicates that Britain's indiscriminate and not particularly profitable arms sales are an escape from hard decisions about rationalizing industry and work-sharing with other countries, in terms of international security.

On 5 March 1980, sellers and buyers met at the first international exhibition of military wares held in Asia. Malaysia's national stadium, the country's largest indoor sports arena, was crammed with rifles, machine guns, rocket launchers, ammunition for these weapons, the electronic and optical accoutrements of the latest in sophisticated war gear and scale models of tanks, planes, ships and the other vehicles of warfare.

Hughes Aircraft Co. had invited all comers to a multimedia presentation of 'a combination of hardware, mock-ups, and graphics to describe some of the 1,500 programs and products that have made the company a free world leader in the design, development and production of electronic systems for defense'. (*New York Times*, 6 March 1980).

The exposition had been put together by Kiver Communications, a Chicago concern with outposts in Britain, Japan and Singapore that is headed by an American, Milton Kiver, and specializes in trade shows. Although strictly commercial in character, politics had not been avoided. Singapore had been chosen originally, but turned down the request. China wanted to send a large delegation of arms experts but could not obtain Malaysian visas for them. Israel and South Africa wanted to exhibit, but were refused because Malaysia recognizes neither nation. Most of the 230 exhibitors were Western European, with France, Britain and Italy most strongly represented. A broker is reported to have criticized the tight US restrictions on foreign arms sales and said that if curbs were lifted, the United States would redress its unfavourable balance of payments into a positive account!

Why are not the exuberant Japanese exporters mentioned in this list? In 1967 Japan's Ministry of Commerce and Industry promulgated a strict regulation against exportation of 'finished' war materials for sale. But, according to a special report in *Le Monde* (10 April 1980), American armaments and planes are being produced under licence in Japan and negotiations are now proceeding with the United States for the joint production of missiles. A confidential letter, moreover, has been published in the Japanese journal *Mainichi* envisaging Japanese co-operation with NATO, especially Germany. *Le Monde* also reported that a private enterprise plan to export equipment for uranium enrichment to Pakistan had been nipped in the bud by British Secret Service intervention.

(1) Traders in death

The modern arms trade does not stop at the harbours and airports of the importing country: it goes deep inside the nation and imports technicians and massive investment capital as well. This new peril has been described by Michael Klare, of the US Institute for Policy Studies, as a big step up in the transfer of conventional arms, which will actually increase the danger of nuclear war:

> The increasing sophistication of weapons permits deeper penetration of enemy territory, making more civilian targets vulnerable sooner, thus increasing the likelihood of quick escalation to nuclear conflagration. The chances that the nuclear powers will be drawn into a local conflict increase as more and more of their technicians operate at critical nerve centers to service the weaponry increase.

The following figures of the value of exports of armaments give some idea of the value of this trade:

Country	$ million
US	38,257
USSR	22,053
France	3,819

106

Country	$ million
UK	2,832
China	2,163
FRG	1,958
Czechoslovakia	1,391
Canada	1,273
Poland	1,141
Italy	1,093
Others	3,090
Total	79,070

(Source: Arms Control and Disarmament Agency, 1978)

Mr Klare cited the notorious Iranian arms transactions as an example of this invasion of American carpetbaggers. For each billion dollars spent by Iran for arms, 40 per cent went for weaponry and 60 per cent for technical services. The F-14 Tomcat, for example, would require one Iranian pilot and 20 *American* computer technicians to service the plane for 24 hours, for each hour logged in the air. The Iranian revolution caught many of these unfortunate Americans off base. 'In the hectic arms trade with Iran in the 1970s,' states the *Washington Post* (26 January 1980), 'the broad security interests of the US Government were confused – and sometimes overwhelmed – by the personal financial interests of American weapons merchants who swarmed to Teheran. The Shah, Mohammed Reza Pahlavi, complained that he sometimes was unable to tell whether various weapons systems were promoted to further US policy or to generate profits for US defense contractors and fees for their representatives.'

The Shah was reported to have said: 'You Americans pretend to be so righteous . . . But it's hard for me to believe that your MAAG officers (the military advisory group at the US Embassy) haven't already been hired by American companies and aren't under their influence . . . Are they giving me real advice or just promoting companies?' This throws a lurid light on what happened to the US Embassy when the revolution swept the Shah away.

Documents, contracts and interviews between US and Iranian officials, military men and businessmen have since portrayed a booming arms trade, hard-sell techniques, questionable payments and possible conflicts of interest, all of which raised the cost of the weapons to the Iranian Government. As one example of the cheating surrounding this arms trade, according to one report, the US Justice Department's criminal division is investigating the business activities of a Secretary of Defense's personal adviser in Iran from 1973 to 1975. When the Russians went into Iran's neighbour in 1980, they knew exactly what had been going on next-door. But did anybody else?

Reverting to Mr Klare, he also warned of a new dimension to proliferation: 'By 1985, 30 to 40 nations will have the capacity to produce sophisticated military equipment.' At present, the developed countries are the primary suppliers. For instance, US arms sales between 1973 and 1975 'jumped from 1 billion to 12 billion dollars a year.' This pace continued with the end of the Vietnam War in 1975 and the consequent loss of the domestic market for arms. Moreover, with the poor balance of payments due to spiralling oil prices, the US has actively sought foreign arms markets, especially in the Middle East, as shown above. The aforementioned *Le Monde* revelations underline America's anxiety to 'assist' China to obtain the Mitzubishi T-74 tank.

Another arms analyst, Anthony Sampson, author of *The Arms Bazaar* (1978) takes the British Government especially to task. He says:

The language of the British Government arms salesmen is as zealous as that of any highpowered huckster, with an added element of military confidence. A recent hearty briefing note from Army Marketing urges customers to join 'the club' by advertising in the official arms catalogue (kept secret from the public), and offers to rent space on the naval floating exhibition which will sail to Africa and Latin America in September.

Of course, the British can always pass the blame on to the Americans, *who are responsible for more than half the world's arms trade*. And it is true that under President Carter the US is guilty of similar contradictions. The President came into office insisting that his country cannot be both the world's leading arms salesman and the leading spokesman for peace; but America is still both.

It is, of course, easier still to pass the blame on to Third World countries. They resent, as an infringement of their new-found sovereignty, any attempt by arms suppliers to control their imports, and will always threaten to buy from the Soviet bloc. But this cannot absolve the supplying of megamurder technology as a 'special responsibility' of the British, as Mr Callaghan told the 1978 UN Special Session. This moral issue has to be faced, for the figures on our charts show that the West is leading the Russians *far ahead* in this disgraceful abrogation of the United Nations Charter and the disarmament proposals to which Britain has put its signature. Hamstrung though Britain is by being shackled to the NATO war-chariot, there is still one path to integrity and freedom along which the British people can resolutely lead the whole United Nations and that is to abandon and renounce *unilaterally* this 'bloody traffic' as a crime against mankind.

The word 'unilateral' seems to frighten the supporters of a continuing arms race. But all decisions by a responsible democratic government *must* be unilateral. The 1980–81 Defence White Paper calls on the British taxpayers to hot up the arms race 3½ per cent and 3 per cent each year up to 1985, because £10¾ *billion* is not enough. How do we break through this vicious spiral of unilateral decisions except by unilateral decisions to cut it at as many points as possible?

(2) Profiteers proliferate

While in the last ten years the total world military expenditure has greatly increased, its distribution for various regions has been changing. For example, whereas in 1967 NATO and the WAPO spent 81 per cent of the total military expenditure and the Third World (excluding China) spent about 6 per cent, these figures had grown by 1977 to 71 per cent and 14 per cent respectively. Figure 6 shows changes in the military expenditure of various regions over the same ten-year period. It can be seen

109

that the greatest changes have occurred in the Middle Eastern countries and Africa. In fact, between 1971 and 1976 military expenditure in the Middle East region has increased threefold, for the reasons explained in later chapters. Africa continues to spend a considerable amount of its resources on the military and has doubled such expenditure *since 1973*.

An enormous proportion of financial resources devoted to military activities is spent by the four major suppliers. It is ironic that these four – the United States, the Soviet Union, the United Kingdom and France – have been spasmodically involved in efforts to curb the proliferation of nuclear weapons, yet have made no concerted attempt to tackle the spread of conventional weapons. (We say 'spasmodically' because in May 1980 President Carter recommended that the US Nuclear Regulatory Commission approve sales of 38 tons of enriched uranium to India.) However, a start was made in 1977 by the US and the USSR, with a joint working group on the control of conventional transfers.

At the end of World War II, only four countries – the US, the UK, the Soviet Union and Canada – had any significant capacity to produce major weapons (aircraft, armoured vehicles and ships); but, by 1977, some 48 countries were producing major weapons. The United States, however, ran into a fierce dilemma in blocking proliferation. The Shah of Iran had told Washington in July 1978 that he wanted to spend $2 billion for 70 more F-14 fighter planes. His request put additional strain on President Carter's promise to *reduce* foreign arms sales. This issue was not surprising, as former President Nixon, the Shah's personal friend, had promised the Shah practically everything he asked for! The *Washington Post* report, cited above, contained this choice piece of reporting:

A former MAAG official recalls a session during which the Shah leafed through the definitive international manual on naval vessels, *Jane's Fighting Ships*, tapping the multimillion-dollar vessels he wanted. 'It was as if he was going through a Sears, Roebuck catalogue,' the US official said. However, the Shah was displeased with the huge arms commissions in which some of his top generals and members of his family participated, albeit secretly.

110

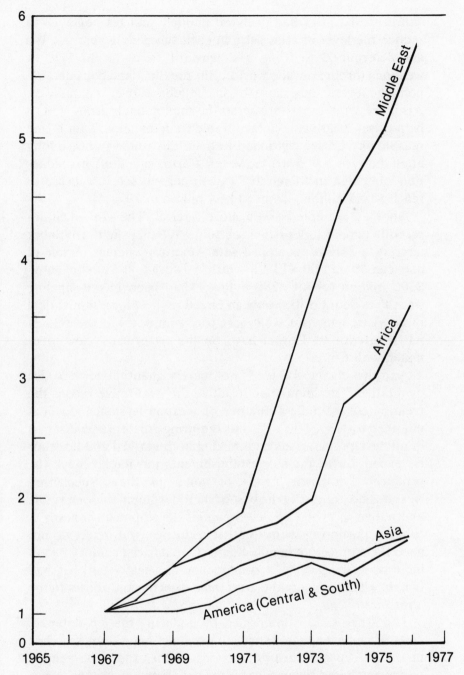

Fig.6   Changes in military expenditure (at 1973 prices and exchange rates) of various regions since 1967. The 1967 military expenditure values of each region were taken as a unity.
Source: SIPRI Yearbook 1978

111

President Carter had declared publicly that his policy is 'to reduce the level of arms sales in each succeeding year . . . We are determined to bring a downward trend in the sale of weapons throughout the world.' But the Shah had considerable political leverage because of his influence over oil policies. Also, the United States wanted the money badly from Iran to help offset its growing unfavourable trade balance. That is one reason why Carter continued to back this runaway horse long after the race was over! However, Carter called off his reduction campaign in March 1980, with current sales expected to reach $14.5 billion – from $11.34 billion in 1977.

Another example is even more farcical. The United States recently agreed to let Israel sell some 50 KFIR fighter-bomber aircraft to *Taiwan*, equipped with American engines. A sale of between 50 and 60 KFIR aircraft to Taiwan, at a cost of some $500 million (about £280 million), had been in the pipeline since President Ford *rejected* an Israeli request for a similar deal three years ago. But what sort of an impact will the sale of KFIR aircraft to Taiwan have on the Americans' new love-match with China?

And this maniacal trade is not merely quantitative. It is also qualitative. The immediate result of the qualitative race is the creation of an endless number of weapon 'systems'. Each is intended for a specific task, thus requiring greater specialization in military preparations and making both vertical and horizontal expansion of military establishments inevitable. Since the producers' domestic needs of some of these specialized weapons do not justify the cost of their development, one viable alternative to giving up new weapons development honestly is to sell a portion of them to other countries, who really do not need them or cannot handle them. (One African country had to build special roads to accommodate the heavy tanks it had bought.) This is where the arms *trade* directly contributes to the arms *race*.

The arms trade is intensified by financing the development costs of new weapons systems, on the one hand, thus speeding up obsolescence of existing weapons, on the other. The weapon that is purchased today pays for the development of its superior, thus contributing to its own uselessness. Moreover, specialized armaments are changing so fast that even the superpowers cannot afford to procure more than a limited number of units from each system. The arms race has recently become, therefore, more a scramble for variety than a race for quantity. To the basic task of killing *people* has been added the new task of killing *weapons*!

Another important by-product of this technological arms binge is that major domestic arms production is impossible except for a few industrialized states. This leaves the great majority of developing countries in the awkward position of dependence on the rich man's arms trade for their biggest 'security' needs. Dependence on foreign weapons and technology leads almost always to political dependence. Iran, America's faithful ally in the Persian Gulf, provides an example. There were over a thousand Americans working on or in the Shah's new military air fleet alone. And more and more would have had to go there soon after, along with the other sophisticated equipment he ordered. All this was going on behind thousand-mile frontier with the Soviet Union. What were the Russians thinking? The Iran revolution was a shocker to everybody, Russians included. When in January 1980, the Russian tanks swept into the country next door – Afghanistan – President Carter made speeches·about what happened in Prague in 1968. We all read about this comparison in all the newspapers, too. But the 1968 and 1980 events could not have been more disparate. Carter did not happen to remember so clearly what had happened in Iran in the 1970s. This *lapsus memoriae* does not justify what happened in Afghanistan, of course, but it warns us that ducks and drakes can live so close together that it is difficult to distinguish between them. The war-hawks in Washington were busy building up their potentials in the Persian Gulf *before* Russia sent troops to Afghanistan under the terms of Clause 4 of the Afghan/USSR Treaty of Friendship.

Still another disturbing consequence of the qualitative arms race is its role in heightening insecurity and tensions, thereby making pre-emptive strikes more likely and wars more destructive. To appreciate the destructiveness of modern weapons one does not, however, need to wait for their deployment in combat. They perform their destructive functions during peace-time by diverting human, material, and financial resources from urgent economic and social tasks (see next chapter) into these extravagant and criminal devices for destroying life on this planet. For that reason alone, our repudiation of the arms race must be clear, absolute and unequivocal.

The Brandt Commission in February 1980, in its unusually frank report on international development, was convinced that 'more arms are not making mankind safer, only poorer'. Total military expenditure is approaching $450,000m a year (about £200,000m), of which more than half is spent by the United States and Russia. Annual spending on official development aid is only $20,000m. 'If only a fraction of the money, manpower and research at present devoted to military uses were diverted to development, the future prospects of the Third World would look entirely different,' they concluded.

One of the most brilliant and outspoken leaders against the arms race and the jingoistic manoeuvres that boost it is Alfonso Garcia Robles, UN Ambassador of Mexico, who pointed out to the Committee on Disarmament in Geneva on 4 February 1980: 'The origins of current events were not as simple as the mass media would have the world believe. These events [referring to Afghanistan] had deep roots and varied ramifications, including factors which were imponderable . . . What the world was witnessing today was a continuing escalation of measures and countermeasures by the Big Powers to exert pressure.'

It is because short-term political leaders make short-term political judgments, while 'off-the-cuff' TV judgments are no judgments at all, that the ordinary public are trapped in a snakepit of fear and ignorance, aware of their peril, but not knowing where to turn to escape. For this reason, the later pages of this book call for an intensive campaign in disarmament and peace education of a fundamental character.

(3) Overselling the Third World

Since 1945, nearly all the wars fought in odd corners of the world have been in the Third World. The Third World is rapidly being transformed into a battleground, where local disputes over boundaries are being turned into proxy wars of East *v.* West. *Three-quarters of the international arms trade is now with the Third World*. It is fast on the increase. The number of aircraft, missiles, armoured vehicles and warships supplied to the Third World in the last six years is equal to that sent in the previous twenty. Jonathan Power (*IHT*, 15 June 1978) draws attention to another comparison: 'The West, during the period of 1970–76 provided 60 per cent of sub-Saharan African arms imports: the Russians only 30 per cent and the Chinese 10 per cent. These sales are increasing at the rate of 12 per cent a year, far above the rate of economic growth of even the fastest-growing developing countries. Africa itself is increasing its purchases at the rate of 20 per cent annually.'

Since the Third World patterns its armies on those of the industrialized states, these costs will continue to escalate. Weapon systems are becoming more intricate, and more expensive – and obsolescence sets in quicker as every year goes by. Long-range surface-to-air missiles were sold to one developing nation in 1958; but to 27 in 1975. Supersonic aircraft went to one developing nation in 1957; but to 43 in 1975.

Seventy per cent of US arms exports go to the Middle East. Sales of new weapons to Iran and Saudi Arabia started with President Nixon and were continued by his successors. This colossal lethal input into a future World War III battlefield on the southern borders of Russia has been justified not only on grounds of 'national security' but by an impoverished United States (as stated above) in search of petrodollars. The biggest scandal of all is Saudi Arabia's defence expenditure of $2000 *per capita* – the highest on earth! One of Lockheed's executives said that they were *expecting* military conscription there when the Prince Sultan suddenly announced it. (*IHT Special Supplement*, February 1980).

According to the Stockholm International Peace Research Institute, the United States is the largest arms salesman to the Third World, with 38 per cent of the world's total. Britain and France, however, are providing another 18 per cent. Yet selling conventional killers is a cruel way of winning friends and influencing people. Governments find, however, that it is quicker and easier to administer an arms programme than one of economic aid, as evidenced by the Brandt Commission.

This is the old question of priorities. Priorities of what? Human needs or inhuman profits? The Russians also seem to prefer it that way, but with less hypocrisy. In Africa, the Soviet

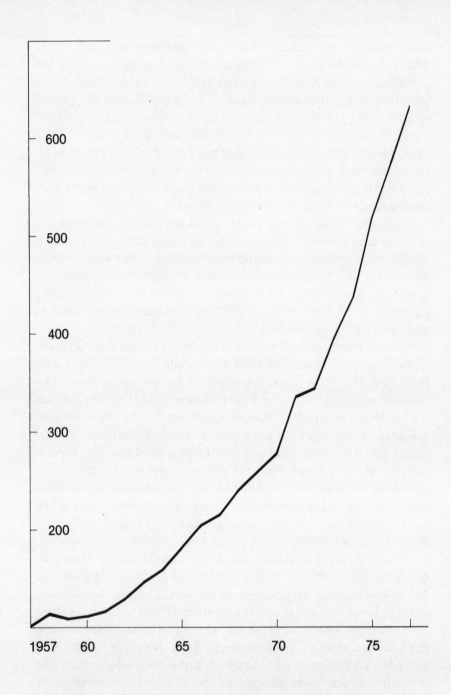

Fig.7   Rate of increase of military expenditure in the Third World, 1957–77 (constant 1973 prices, 1957 = 100).
Source: SIPRI data

116

Union spends about three times more on guns than butter. Its incursion into Afghanistan is running up further bills, and even losing its bread as well as the butter, since the US cut off grain sales.

Back home, in America, however, all is a close secret. The death trade feeds a lot of Americans, but the press concentrates on 'the Soviets'. Apart from the notorious twin giants who run America's war machine – Lockheed and Northrop – there are also EXXON, General Motors, and ITT currently involved in 58 *billion* dollars global sales. But they never mention anything about overseas arms contracts. Even Singer Sewing Machines are in the H-Bomb business.

For this vast conglomerate empire, which virtually pressures the election of local delegates to Congress, the US Government is just an agent, not a master. So 'arms control' has no tangible meaning. In fact, the Northrop Corp., whose proposed F-18 fighter plane is now under challenge, has increased its lobbying team in Washington, while remaining solidly hooked into the 'old boy network' of military officers. 'The political spectrum of the aerospace firm's new lobby team now stretches from a Georgia connection, Joel Paris (Georgia's National Guard Director when President Carter was governor) to the new-style, low-key lobbyist William Timmons, formerly President Nixon's liaison with Congress.' (*Washington Post*, 18 July 78).

The manner by which Northrop is still hooked into the 'old boy network', however, was shown by a recent Pentagon run-down of retired and former military officers on the payrolls of defence contractors. Northrop had 61 former military officers in its employ, just triple the number on the payroll of McDonnell-Douglas, the aerospace contractor that actually got most of the defence contracts in 1977. Before the US-supported Shah was knocked down in 1979, Teheran was chock full of Pentagon 'old boys' as we have seen, funnelling petrodollars into the maws of American arms merchants. The so-called students outside the US Embassy were furious – and still are – but they locked up some of the wrong Americans.

What is the effect of this terrible example of industrializing the local warlords of the 'poor' half of the world? It means two basic things. First, it means this:

The blunt fact is that the developing countries are contributing *proportionately* more to the rise in spending on arms than the super-powers. Their share rose from 6 per cent in 1966 to 15 per cent in 1976, and there is no sign of a let-up. Admittedly they are aided and abetted by the salesmen and governments of the developed world, including those of Britain. The point is simply that everyone contributes to the problem, so that everyone must contribute to its remedy. (*The Times*, 3 July 1978).

The other basic fact – overlooked by the champions of 'free enterprise' – is that the under-nourished and under-housed half of mankind is being despoiled of its natural resources and turned into a market for mutual destruction, so that the West's military hierarchy can continue to live in opulence at their expense. So where do we start? With the sellers? Or with the buyers? With the rich? Or with the poor?

Yet this depressing story of military plutocracy is not without the stirrings of conscience. Several British voluntary agencies and peace groups –Campaign Against the Arms Trade, International Voluntary Service, Oxfam, Pax Christi, Volunteer Action and War on Want – have formed the Committee on Poverty and the Arms Trade (COPAT) and have attacked successive British Governments for their involvement in arms sales to the world's poorest nations.

They point out that these arms sales are shown to retard or even reverse the process of development. A tragic cycle of poverty-repression-militarization is created. Scarce foreign exchange is wasted, land is taken out of food production to produce exports to gain more foreign currency. The peasantry are dispossessed, becoming workers on starvation wages. Such societies become increasingly dependent on an alien, expensive and unproductive technology. COPAT agencies are urging that the British Government work with management and trade unions to convert the British arms industry to socially valuable production.

In a later chapter we pursue further this assertion of a public conscience in terms of specific proposals for dismantling the war machine. Meanwhile, Britain can begin by proposing that the 1982 Special Session set up a Disarmament Authority (which might be structured along the lines of the proposed Sea Bed Authority) or the expansion of the present UN Disarmament Commission with adequate technical staff to assist governments to switch their arms budgets to development. Could there be a better use of that eight thousand million pounds – plus its equivalent in dollars and roubles?

V
Wasted Billions

We have already seen that armaments are a contributory cause of inflation in any economy, i.e. they drive up consumer prices, simply because consumers can't consume armaments, but they have to pay for them. So let us now look at some facts and figures.

Let us start with the 'wobbly dollar'. In the summer of 1978 it 'fell' (as the saying is) to one and a half to an English pound from four dollars to the pound before NATO appeared. This is not cause and effect, of course; but one reality is that the countries of Western Europe have progressively gained in wealth since the end of World War II, while the US share of world economic power has proportionally declined. European nations have undertaken relatively few military responsibilities *outside* their continent and none has felt powerful enough to play a world role nor serve as full accessory to US policy, though the US Congress is constantly pressuring its NATO allies to 'share' the heavy US burden in Europe. So 'Europe' (that means five Western nations) has to pay for the 572 extra-special warheads that the Pentagon is clamping on them for the 1980s. Reasoning that WAPO would take advantage of the diversion of US forces to the Persian Gulf, the Defense Department was anxious in April 1980 for NATO to rev up its ammunition stocks.

The powerful United States, which came out of World War II with flying colours, i.e. having gained in production, trade, and investments *from* that war, has since 1945 poured its wealth, manpower and resources into the still unfinished struggle in Korea and the unspeakable costs and miscalculations in South-East Asia, as well as into European 'defence', always chasing the will-o'-the-wisp of communism, and thereby hardening the latter's appeal to weaker nations. It is a strange irony that, today, the mighty dollar cannot look the resurgent yen in the face, since – among other reasons – Japan is bound by treaty to limit its military commitments to virtually domestic safety purposes.

A further factor is the US *dependence* on the developing world. Since the 1960s a new phase of Third World thinking has persuaded many Americans to say 'We need a less militaristic approach in US Foreign policy.' We quote here Professor Glenn A. McLain, a former consultant on International and Balkan Affairs, US Department of State, who has said: 'As rich as America is in natural resources, we now import over two-thirds of our needs in six major minerals: bauxite, chromium, cobalt, magnesium, nickel and tin. Naturally, these, like our needs in oil resources, are essential to the creative business and military planners in the United States.' And he adds:

All of these minerals are found in the countries of the Third World. These and others used by America in international trade in 1976 alone amounted to $28.5 billions. These important economic facts highlight the continuing importance of the Third World in future strategic planning by American government, business and military leaders. (*The Churchman*, October 1979).

Economics is a treacherous subject. But in spite of the Western governments' attempts to switch the blame on the oil crisis and much else *outside* their control, some facts cannot be contradicted. The first is that the arms race has pushed up the price of practically every item in your food basket. You can't buy a nuclear submarine; but your tax money has to buy it! In the unemotional language of a detailed documented report produced for the information of all governments by the United Nations, we read:

High military expenditures sustained over a long period of

121

time are likely to aggravate upward pressures on the price level in several ways. First, military expenditures are inherently inflationary in that purchasing power and effective demand is created without an offsetting increase in immediately consumable output or in productive capacity to meet future consumption requirements. This excess demand creates an upward pressure on prices throughout the economy . . . Second, there are reasons to believe that the arms industry offers less resistance to increases in the cost of labour and of the other factors of production than do most other industries, partly because of its highly capital- and technology-intensive character and partly because cost increases in this sector can more readily be passed on to the customer . . . Finally, and more generally, the diversion of substantial capital away from the civilian sector impedes the long-term growth of productivity and thereby renders the economy more vulnerable to inflationary pressures.*

The British Government's 1980/81 defence White Paper, for example, expressed constant 'disturbance' and 'concern' over the rising costs – 35 years after the last war ended – of maintaining troops of the British Army on the Rhine. Actually they are no longer on the Rhine (as this author clearly recollects they were when he was hiking with a rucksack on his back *before* the Second World War!), but they are still costing the British taxpayer £763,000,000. Such costs have risen, so the White Paper admits, by an annual 3½ per cent in real terms over the last 20 years.

Of course, all this is due to the 'continuing growth of the Warsaw Pact forces beyond what is needed for their own defence'; but the White Paper is less explicit as to what *is* needed for WAPO's defence. Later in this book, we take up the French Government's proposal to convene an all-Europe Disarmament Conference. This may help the British, as well as WAPO, to define the kind of defence they mutually 'need'. It is about time that somebody pricked this inflated balloon miscalled 'defence'.

*Economic and Social Consequences of the Arms Race and of Military Expenditures, UN, New York, 1978

(1) Budgeting for Armageddon

In 1970 the nations of the world were spending $200 billion a year on armaments. The total had by 1978 doubled to $400 billion. It is now getting every day closer to $500 – that is at a rate of more than *a billion dollars a day*! The size of regular armed forces increased to 23 million in 1978, 2 million more than in 1970 and 7 million more than in 1960. It is still growing and costing mankind more and more in diverted economic investment. NATO's decision to *increase* present spending of 3 per cent *over inflation*, is the act of a drunken driver going full speed along the edge of a precipice.*

Washington last year passed funds for another nuclear-powered carrier and a $119.3 billion defence appropriations bill that was described as the largest money measure ever put before Congress. Three of the Navy's fleet of thirteen carriers are nuclear-powered; a fourth nuclear carrier is under construction. Supporters of nuclear-powered carriers argued that they are needed to 'offset' growing Soviet naval strength. The usual refrain. The race between the US and USSR navies is one of the newest and most dangerous phases of the arms race. Such vessels are extremely mobile targets, Senators have said, yet equivalent to overseas bases, of which the US already has hundreds.

But opponents of more nuclear-powered carriers argued that they are 'sitting ducks' in a nuclear age. They cost up to three times as much as conventional carriers. 'Does anybody think that the building of a new nuclear carrier will deter war with the Soviet Union?' asked Representative George Mahon, chairman of the House Appropriations Committee, who opposed the new carrier. But 'We need a platform from which to project our power,' Rep. Richard White said (repeat: *'project our power'*!),

---

* If the present Government adheres to its stated policy of increasing arms spending in real terms by 3 per cent each year during this Parliament, then (neglecting inflation) Britain's arms bill will rise as follows:

1979–80	£9,100 m
1980–81	£9,373 m
1981–82	£9,654 m
1982–83	£9,944 m
1983–84	£10,242 m
1984–85	£10,549 m

123

noting that the number of US military bases abroad had shrunk from more than 100 to fewer than 30 in recent years. The Senator must have missed some fifty countries. There are 26 bases in Turkey alone, but in May 1980 the Turks insisted on joint control over the keys.

The major industrial nations are now exporting military weapons worth $8 billion a year to the poor developing countries, as we saw above – three times as much as in 1970 and four times as much as in 1960. Why so continuous a growth? Since the 1970s, the United States and the Soviet Union have increased their *stockpiles* of nuclear warheads from 8,000 to 14,000. (We say 'stockpiles' because all this is totally useless junk, and must remain so – of no *economic* value.) Other nuclear powers, Britain, France, China, India (and probably Israel) have another 500 deliverable nuclear weapons. This is before the 572 extra begin to arrive. And all sensible people in all countries without exception are hoping that they *will never be used*. So why not stop *NOW*?

Over three decades, a large military establishment has become a permanent fixture in the economies of most of the major powers. Millions of people, in and out of uniform, are employed in the dubious business of preparing for World War III, *without any belief in it*! This is quite a new psychological situation for military leaders to face. Yet in many countries all over the world, the arms race has become a substitute way of life. In addition to those directly involved in producing, maintaining and operating the instruments of war, millions of civilians are being told that they owe their economic security to the arms race.

Many cities in close proximity to arsenals, airfields, weapons manufacturing plants, and other military bases do, of course, derive a major part of their livelihood from military spending. Yet the inability of the United States to maintain full employment in peace-time is well known. West Germany, with a much more modest military budget, however, has suffered less inflation and unemployment than the United States in recent years. Japanese military expenditures are less than one per cent of the gross national product, and its economy is at maximum strength, even after the impact of quadrupled oil prices on a nation *totally dependent on imported oil*.

124

What these facts make clear is that high military expenditures compel a nation to spend a great deal of its resources in profitless, dangerous and ruinously expensive armaments and to do so at the expense of the long-term economic well-being of its citizens. According to the US economist, Arthur F. Burns, a war economy may appear to bring full employment, but it can never bring prosperity: 'To the extent that we allocate labour, materials, and capital to national defence, we cannot satisfy our desires for other things.'

On 24 July 1978 the US Arms Control and Disarmament Agency reported that the nations of the world are spending more than $750,000 *a minute* for military purposes. The (then) $400 billion total was two and a half times the amount the world spent on public health. The United States and the Soviet Union accounted for two-thirds of the weapons exported to other nations, *with the Middle East the biggest customer*. The United States exported 39 per cent of the arms sold abroad and the Soviet Union 28 per cent. The fighting in Africa is manifested in the Agency's report by sharp increases in weapons imports by countries there. African military expenditures climbed from $1.4 billion in 1967 to $5.9 billion in 1976.

'In the fiscal year just ended,' says the *Washington Post*, 'the United States sold $13.6 billion worth of weapons and military services abroad – a record that a President who campaigned fervently against such transactions is hardly inclined to boast about.' (7 October 1978).

Yet the hawks are always pushing him on for still more! 'I know from experience,' said a certain frank and astute politician, 'that the leaders of the armed forces can be very persistent in claiming their share, when it comes time to allocate funds. Every commander has all sorts of very convincing arguments why he should get more than anyone else. Unfortunately there's a tendency for people who run the armed forces to be greedy and self-seeking. They're always ready to throw in your face the slogan: "If you try to economize on the country's defences today, you'll pay in blood when war breaks out tomorrow." ' (Quoted from *Khrushchev Remembers*, 1970).

Almost all regions of the world throughout the 1967–76 period, even after the adjustment for inflation, were continuing the upward trend, registered since the end of World War II,

125

according to Paul Warnke, a very enlightened former head of the Arms Control Agency. He said that his last report was done 'to stimulate informed attention' to the growing arms trade and the 'scarce resources' it was consuming. These items summarize his findings:

(1) One tax dollar [or pound] in six now goes to the arms race;

(2) The average family pays more in taxes to support the arms race than to educate their children;

(3) Nuclear bomb inventories of the two superpowers, already sufficient to destroy every city in the world seven times over, are growing at the rate of three nuclear bombs a day;

(4) Developing nations now have one soldier for 250 inhabitants; one doctor for 3,700;

(5) Modern technology makes it possible to deliver a bomb across the world in minutes; women in rural areas of Asia and Africa walk several hours a day for the family's water supply;

(6) Developing nations use five times more foreign exchange for arms imports than for agricultural machinery;

(7) UN peacekeeping forces around the world spend $135 million yearly; national military forces *3,000 times as much*.

Nevertheless, in Washington a group of former national security officials has called for a $260 billion increase in military spending over the next six years 'to restore the nation's capacity to deter and contain Soviet expansion'. The Committee on the Present Danger asserts that 'for more than 10 years this country has neither provided adequately for the common defense nor protected its economic stability'. The group presented a plan for bolstering the Carter administration's programme for military spending by $260 billion through fiscal year 1985. In the light of the foregoing figures this committee is evidently determined to turn the present danger into a future disaster.

(2) What to do with arms money

Professor Seymor Melman of Columbia University, a long-time authority on the US military economy, has said:

Since 1951, the military budget has exceeded the total net

126

profit of all corporations every year. The net profits of all corporations are understood as a potential capital fund. The military budget comprises a sum of money large enough and of a composition of skilled manpower and materials to be understood as a capital fund. *So the largest capital fund in the US since 1951 has been the military budget.* [Our italics].

Another critical variable is technology. And for the last quarter century, every year, the US Government has dominated research and development. Federal governmental expenditures have ranged from 66 to 80 per cent by military and related enterprises. The importance of capital and technology is that they dominate production. Without productive capability a community cannot live. In order to live, a community must produce. But this cannot be taken for granted in the face of a long war economy, because the elementary resources for production, that is, capital and technology and the presence of manpower, are pre-empted. There *has* to be a deleterious effect. Precisely that is now taking place in America.

James Treires, Staff Economist in the Washington Center for Defense Information, has stated: 'It must be made clear that the requirements of peace will guide economic policies toward full employment and stable prosperity. Men and women who now produce aircraft, bombs and tanks can just as easily produce subway cars, homes and solar heaters. But these simple economic facts do not translate easily into effective programmes. Political struggles, ideological abstractions and entrenched interests may greatly complicate the transition.'

In each nation, in fact, a different set of government actions will be required to ease the transition from the frantic arms race of today to a more relaxed international climate in which meeting the material and spiritual needs of its citizens will become the dominant theme. Despite this variability in national cultures and economic circumstances, a few basic principles should, according to James Treires, guide government policy:

(1) Full employment must be guaranteed by the central government. It is now accepted in the United States that support of the jobs and economic security of the defence sector is a legitimate concern of the Federal Government. It is time now to demand the *same right* for workers in private employment;

(2) Income distribution must be a major concern of governments. Extreme inequalities are a threat to the long-term stability of any government;

(3) Responsibility for major decisions about the allocation of capital investment must be assumed by all democratic governments, acting in concert with private economic interests;

(4) As education sweeps over ever-wider areas of the globe, the earth's citizens will learn to demand of their elected leaders what every human being wants most – peace and security, not merely to endure but to enjoy life – so that the energies now consumed in the arms race may be diverted to the public good.

Ruth Leger Sivard, the pioneer American researcher in this field, seeking for alternatives, says: 'For a poverty-scarred world, the vista of economic and social opportunities that disarmament can offer is dazzling. What could $400 billion a year, or even a fraction of it, if turned away from death and destruction, do to succour and enrich the lives of all people on earth? The potential is so vast as to seem beyond comprehension.'

In fact, at today's rate of military spending, a fraction no larger than five per cent of that budget could translate into food and shelter for millions of people; it could mean hospitals and schools where there are none; cleaner air and water; children saved from crippling malnutrition, blindness, preventable disease; the poorest one-third of humanity able for the first time to live with hope of normal, productive lives.

Mrs Sivard points out, however, that before the world can enjoy those benefits, we must find more effective ways to move toward the disarmament goal, and she suggests 'the mutual example approach', as it is called, which endeavours to *lower* the opposing threat rather than racing endlessly to exceed it. 'Mutual example reverses the arms race by using the same procedures that created it: action, observation, reaction. In the build-up of arms, *unilateral* decisions are the normal method and they can be made quickly. They are based on a continuous observation of the moves made by the opposing parties. If the same procedures can be used for the de-escalation of arms, there is hope that a turning point can be reached.' This is the WAR AVOIDANCE policy we are advocating in this book. This is where a Committee on the Present Danger can get to work on real safety.

A glance back in history, Mrs Sivard says, gives some cause for encouragement. A mutual example was tried in the 1960s of restraint by the two superpowers. 'Mutual example' was a Soviet term, but it was the US which, in secret conversations with the USSR in 1963, first raised the matter of informal budgetary restraint. This approach was followed up, still in secret, in 1964, until ruptured abruptly by the American entry into the Vietnam War in 1965. Mutual restraint between the two superpowers can be reflected in what has since been known as 'détente', encouraging stability in their military expenditure.

Again, we meet with the term 'unilateral'. Perhaps it is in the economics area that the 'unilateral' approach to disarmament will prove most feasible and acceptable, though the militarists have spread the illusion that, for *their* particular country, it means giving in to the Russians, appeasement, or some other form of opprobrious weakness. But it is not only the Russians who are looking for a breakthrough in the East/West defence dilemma. Mr Eric Heffer, MP, states: 'In East Europe today the pressures for peace and greater democracy are increasing.' And he draws attention to the movement for a nuclear-free zone in Europe, backed by scientists, economists, academics and trade unionists from all over Europe; and he asserts that such a movement, initiated by the West, 'is bound to help to relax tension, and the arguments advanced by the Soviet Union for repressive measures because of military dangers will diminish'. (*The Times*, 5 May 1980).

(3) Would disarmament cause unemployment?

The truth is leaking out on both sides of the Atlantic that, instead of giving jobs, the arms business has the unhappy knack of losing jobs. Admiral Gene R. La Rocque of the Center for Defense Information, has asked the question: 'Is military spending good for the economy?' and he answered his own question in the following laconic fashion:

(1) Twenty-five years of heavy emphasis on military programmes have created a strong pro-military constituency as concerned about jobs and income as national defense.

(2) Military spending as an economic stimulant is wasteful and inefficient. As a job-creator, it is among the least effective kinds of federal spending.

(3) American manufacturers are losing efficiency and competitiveness in world markets because of diversion of talent, research effort and capital to the arms industry.

(4) The US still relies heavily on wasteful military pump-priming to generate jobs and increase the gross national product.

(5) *Large Pentagon budgets are a major contributor to the continuing huge federal deficits.*

This attitude would, at first blush, seem to ignore what many ordinary people are thinking. For example, when public opinion pollster Samuel Lubell interviewed voters around the country, he heard comments like these: 'It's a hell of a thing to say, but our economy needs a war'; 'Defense spending should be increased to make more jobs for people'; 'If this country didn't have a war, the economy would come apart.'

However, Admiral La Rocque has stuck to his guns and has insisted: 'The idea that military spending can produce prosperity is widely accepted, but difficult to prove. Simple logic tells us that workers, facilities and materials used for military purposes could otherwise have been employed to produce more goods and services for American consumers.'

The American economist, Arthur F. Burns, once Chairman of the Federal Reserve Board, explains this thus: 'The civilian goods and services that are currently *foregone* on account of expenditures on national defence are, therefore, the current *real cost* of the defence establishment.' But there is little doubt, unfortunately, that high unemployment generates more enthusiasm for military spending. Senator William Proxmire has said: 'At a time when we have a large number of people unemployed, that economic argument is probably the most effective argument of all. I think that we would have been able to kill the B-1 plane in the Senate last year, if it hadn't been for the economic argument.'

In recent years, the Pentagon and its contractors have responded to public criticism of their excessive costs and gross waste by aggressive publicity extolling the economic benefits of

130

military spending. Firms, employees, communities and legislators who benefit from particular projects are being persuaded of their *dependence* on local military spending and of what a cut in the military budget could mean to them. It is the losers – taxpayers and industries in other areas – who foot the bills, but have no comparable public relations effort to tell the public about their losses.

Against this attitude, one energetic American non-governmental organization, the Coalition for a New Foreign and Military Policy (Washington), reports that military spending at a rate of $78 billion a year is responsible for the *un*employment of some 907,000 Americans. And every additional billion dollars of Pentagon spending causes the loss of 11,600 jobs in the United States. Why is this? This is because one of the most persistent myths of modern times is that military spending is good for the economy.

This myth is alleged to have begun in 1941. The facts seemed clear: the US then had a Depression, the worst in modern history. Millions were unemployed. Then, war was declared, and 11,000,000 men joined the armed forces. Millions of people went to work in war plants. And the Depression ended. Hence, the conclusion drawn by most Americans was simple: 'World War II ended the Depression, therefore military spending creates employment and is good for the economy.'

No one explained that it was not the war that ended the Depression, but the enormous sums spent by the Federal Government on hiring soldiers and on buying war materials. Sums of this magnitude spent on *anything* would have ended the Depression. 'We could have rebuilt the railroad system, upgraded our supply of housing, and built desperately needed new schools and hsopitals.'

In a booklet entitled *Prosperity Without Guns*, Dr B. G. Lall of the New York State School of Industrial and Labor Relations at Cornell University, analyses the economic impact of reductions in defence spending in the United States. Betty Lall says that:

This booklet has been written to make the public more familiar with the evidence that reductions in military expenditures need not have negative economic effects if *properly planned*

131

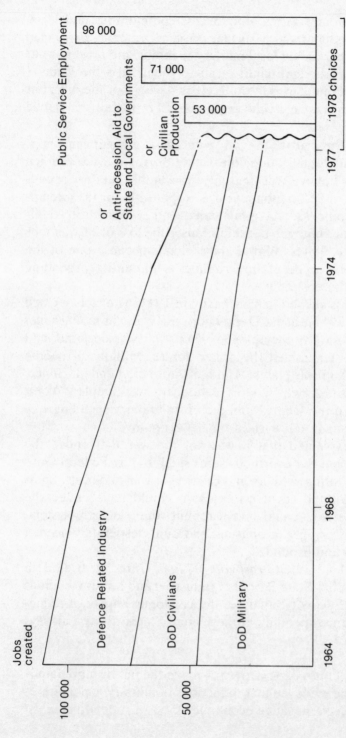

Fig. 8 The vanishing argument for military spending in the USA (*left*). Each year military spending creates fewer jobs, e.g. only 45,800 in 1977, but (*right*) up to twice as many could be created by investment in areas shown.
Source: US Center for Defense Information, based on data from the Department of Defense, Congressional Budget Office and Bureau of Labor Statistics

132

in advance. In fact, while some communities, labour, and businesses may experience temporary difficulties due to conversion, the evidence is that within a few years the net impact on the economy can be positive.

She points out that many Americans are unaware of the work of already established federal agencies that have been helping communities faced with plant or base shutdowns. Many also are unfamiliar with studies which demonstrate that dollar for dollar, 'most non-military spending generates more jobs than military spending'. Though economic changes resulting from arms control or disarmament cannot occur overnight, for arms control and disarmament agreements take time to negotiate, this transfer time could be used to prepare for the expected changes. Thus the necessary adjustments would not be difficult and benefits would soon be felt by all sectors of the population.

Dr Lall explains that during the conversion process many workers in the arms industries would have to make readjustments, so that things cannot be left to chance. But plans are needed to arouse business, labour, government, and communities to contract cutbacks so that the temporary hardships for the most vulnerable can be mitigated.

On the financial side, she explains that the largest single item in the federal budget, which comes out of general tax revenues, is defence. For the fiscal year 1978 $116.4 billion or *nearly 25 per cent of the total budget* was allocated to military spending. This military budget included expenditures for military research and development (R & D) and absorbed over half of all government funds spent on R & D. As a result, it is estimated that *almost half* of the nation's scientific and engineering talent devotes its efforts to military affairs.

But substantial cuts in military spending would not only affect employment directly related to the military. There would be a 'ripple effect' within a community where defence plants are located, so that construction, retail, and service employment would be affected. Firms doing subcontracting could also be affected when defence contracts are cut, and could direct their energies to *permanent* markets.

Studies of workers in US military industries laid off in the past have shown, however, that such workers receive higher pay than their counterparts in civilian employment. This has become a problem in taking civilian jobs, with substantial pay cuts. Conversely, communities, faced by the closing of military-oriented plants, strive to preserve jobs and maintain economic activity generally. Most communities have not anticipated, at this point of general arms build-ups, a loss of military contracts, nor planned how they would replace jobs and business lost. But those that *have* planned have been able to overcome adverse effects much more rapidly than others. The lag between the time of lay-offs in private plants and recovery of employment in the community appears to be about five years.

Since broad government economic programmes are not likely to be very helpful to specific communities in the short run, disarmament planning must therefore involve local communities afflicted with cutbacks. A regional rather than a single town or city approach is frequently the best way of tackling the problem in the United States. Several towns within a county might work together. A financing mechanism might be provided by the pooling of resources of local banks and savings and loan associations and might involve a loan from a government development agency. Has anybody in Britain at government level worked on this conversion problem as Dr Lall and many other Americans, known to the author, have done?

Turning to the United Kingdom, it is of special interest in conversion of war to peace industry to notice how national policy is related to local trade union initiative. Dr Mary Kaldor, Fellow of Sussex University, takes a more fundamentalist position and believes that the government can only act as an investor and reverse the direction of existing policies, if current organizational structures are changed along these lines:

(1) nationalization of some sectors of the defence industry, including the profitable civilian sectors, such as offshore engineering;

(2) workers' participation in the nationalized industries, in order to generate ideas for alternative products and shift the central direction of government policymaking;

(3) planning agreements with all private armaments companies, in order to ensure that capacity is freed from armaments production and that profits from armaments are invested in suitable projects in Britain rather than abroad.

134

It is when we come to the reality of staff sackings and redundancies, however, that recent British experience has something concrete to offer. Two areas involved in armaments manufacture can be briefly surveyed here as pointers to the broad canvas that conversion will have to cover when governments begin to take seriously their pledge of general and complete disarmament. A report by a Labour Party Defence Study Group in 1977 (*Sense about Defence*) gives this example among many:

An ASW Cruiser is being built by the Vickers Shipbuilding Group at Barrow-in-Furness. The group employs around 13,000 workers and has an annual output of £64 million. The cruiser takes up about a fifth of Barrow's shipbuilding capacity. Over its lifetime it will involve 7,000 to 8,000 man years of work. A further 28,000 to 32,000 man years will be taken up in the supplying industries – steel, marine equipment, etc.

This report looks at two aspects of the problem – technical and political – and it makes specific recommendations of relevance to defence conversion. It shows that the conversion potential of the resources engaged in the production of the ASW cruiser is fairly typical of other naval shipyards. The problem of warship conversion is not so different from the problem of *finding* work for surplus capacity in shipbuilding generally. Does the Government's commitment to world peace express itself in specific replanning programmes, or is that left to somebody else?

Vickers Limited is the largest armaments company in Britain, producing the whole range of armaments from small arms to ASW Cruisers and the multi-role combat aircraft. But the shipbuilding process, and the skills and facilities available at Barrow, are commensurate with any kind of large-scale labour-intensive construction which involves heavy metal fabrication and complex logistical problems of supply, storage and scheduling. The possible types of conversion may be broadly divided into three: merchant shipbuilding, alternative land-based manufacturing, and new sea-based technologies.

From the factory floor level, what has become known in Britain as the Lucas Aerospace 'Corporate Plan', is described by its promoters as 'a positive alternative to recession and redundan-

135

cies'. The experience of the Lucas aerospace shop stewards' committee has already become some kind of touchstone. What is remarkable about the Lucas combine is that instead of resisting redundancies, caused by cuts in government defence expenditure, the workforce has suggested the development of *alternative socially useful products* which the market needs and to which the engineers' skills could adapt. The workers' collective ideas have been put into a corporate plan. The technical implications of the plan are being widely discussed in Britain. Both the Transport and General Workers' Union and the Labour Party have made the plan central to their own arguments for the feasibility of defence cuts.

The instigators of this plan use as an example the fact that there are 6,000 kidney failures in Britain every year: 1,000 patients receive transplants, 2,000 are kept ticking over, the other 3,000 go into decline and death. The shortage of kidney machines at Birmingham Hospital, for instance, means that you go into decline if you are under 15 or over 45. The combine wants to produce more and better machines, so a medical team, including practitioners, a bio-engineer and a kidney specialist, has been set up to help them. Moreover, the combine is confronting the Department of Health with needy patients and the information that Lucas Company has the products and the skills to build these machines. Not only would this be real job creation; it might shock the Government out of their lethargy over conversion. The 1980 Defence White Paper is strangely silent about translating British weapons into British welfare.

Mike George, a Research Fellow at the North East London Polytechnic Centre for Alternative Industrial and Technological Systems, says:

In our so-called advanced country we still have millions of sub-standard houses, we lack cheap, efficient heating systems, we are desperately short of some types of medical equipment: but Lucas aerospace workers who could be making these goods are to be thrown onto the dole queue. These workers are demonstrating that a cut in arms production need not result in mass unemployment – it could result in lower unemployment; it could also mean that we start to produce for social need instead of mass annihilation.

136

The two newly established UN Centres for Disarmament (in New York and Geneva) should be authorized and staffed to prepare detailed studies on conversion programmes to assist member states to meet their UN obligations and promises. Under the UN Special Session on Disarmament in 1978 some dozen inter-governmental expert groups have been set up to deal with technical aspects of international arms reduction; but there is no major UN body yet established to advise governments on this basic issue of *conversion* – i.e. how to put the arms race into reverse.

Meanwhile, private groups all over the world are springing into action to pressure their governments (*see Appendix (B)*) to switch from warfare to welfare. One example is the 'Transarm for Survival' campaign in Belgium. It is within this framework that Belgian groups are demanding the blocking of the (military) National Defence Budget and the reallocation of the funds thus acquired for the realization of three complementary objectives:

(1) the reconversion of the arms industry for socially useful purposes;

(2) the investment of funds in the research and implementation of Nonviolent Civilian Defence;

(3) the expansion of development projects put forward and conducted by the Non-governmental Organizations.

VI
Down with Imperialism!

The nostalgic vaudeville song: 'Old soldiers never die, they simply fade away!' cannot be sung today about old empires. They don't die so easily; they simply change their masters. They just drop down a peg or two in status. But these new empires all need plenty of arms – modern ones, and foreign investment money, and mercenaries.

They have become increasingly part of the arms race, prodded on and often paid for by the old empires. The new empires come in all shapes and sizes. But they all aim for the same thing: someone else's territory, his minerals or oil wells. These new style smash-and-grab episodes fill up a lot of hot newspaper and TV space. Africa is the main target. And the big power interlopers all claim that they are in Africa (or Asia) 'by invitation' and insist on being left alone to share the benefits with the private enterprises or military czars back home. That is why the neo-colonies are getting their guns so easily.

The Russians and Cubans are late-comers. But they are now sending in their task forces to direct and train rebel forces. Flash-points of World War III are being multiplied in Africa and the Middle East. They may unexpectedly start off well-laid fuses, so must be watched. We can look at only a few different examples of these smouldering fuses here; but there are many others.

The sheer irony and patent contradictions of some of these

sauve-qui-peut scrambles towards the Indian Ocean (declared a zone of peace by peoples who live around it) became obvious in March 1980 after the Iran and Afghanistan upsets. US officials then began inspecting installations at Berbera, in the Horn of Africa, which had been developed and *actually used* by the Soviet Navy before Somalia put them out in 1977. Meantime, Kenya (next door), being enticed by the same Washington handouts to supply port facilities at Mombasa, has since expressed great apprehension that this build-up of Somalia's militarism will threaten attacks on Kenya as well as Ethiopia.

(1) France invades Zaire

The Organization of African Unity (OAU), though not unified on much else, responded unanimously in Khartoum in July 1978 to French paratroopers dropping on Zaire. OAU adopted a resolution condemning *all* foreign military bases, alliances and pacts in Africa, yet affirming the right of each OAU country to act as it sees fit. It called on member states to 'put an end as soon as possible' to any engagement that runs counter to non-alignment. This is a warning to Americans, Russians, Frenchmen and the rest; certainly to South Africans. The British had (wisely) already got out and later set an example in decolonization in Zimbabwe in 1980, well worthy of emulation by others elsewhere.

France, however, is the only outside power to *admit* having bases in Africa. It has military 'facilities' in Chad, Gabon, Senegal and the Ivory Coast, as well as in tiny Djibouti and the Comoros islands. We will pass over the demise of Bokassa's Central African Empire. French troops were also stationed in Mauritania. Mauritania depended on French warplanes and tanks to wrest the Saharan phosphate away from the Polisarians; but got out in 1979 while the going was good. While Morocco is still using French planes and machines to fight the Polisario, she also used US military planes in June 1978 for an air-lift to bolster Zaire's hold on Katanga's copper mines.

Algeria, Morocco's neighbour, cannot accept what Morocco is doing either in Western Sahara or Zaire. Fortunately, OAU has so far held the ring and kept the peace between them.

139

Morocco will probably soon follow Mauritania and call for quits IF (and it is a big 'if') the United States and France cut off the extra arms. But will they? In October 1979, the Carter Administration reversed its earlier policy towards Morocco and decided to supply King Hassan with new weapons for his campaign against the Polisario, resisting in Western Sahara. The decision produced a prolonged debate between the White House and the State Department. The Moroccans will now be supplied with the DV-10 armed reconnaissance aircraft and the Cobra helicopter gunships they requested more than a year before; but the US then wisely held off.

This shift of policy happily drew Congressional hostility. The chairman of the House Foreign Affairs Sub-committee on Africa said that he would oppose the sale: 'Morocco has been a friend,' he said, 'but friendship does not oblige us to support a war that cannot be won and a course that is not just.' Senator George McGovern held a similar position in the Senate and has expressed his opposition to bolstering this illegal Moroccan annexation of Western Sahara, which the World Court in an advisory opinion unanimously condemned.

Meanwhile, Cuba has maintained an estimated 20,000 soldiers in Angola, but OAU did not regard this as a 'base'. And South African troops were still backing the Portuguese there. Since Cuba was then quarrelling with Moscow (and Castro's independence is proverbial) he first shipped Cubans in two old tubs across the Atlantic without Russia's knowledge, so it is said, to get the Portuguese out of Angola, and succeeded! The OAU could not swallow the Washington line that 'Africa was swarming with Russians'. They said they had met Western colonialists, but not Russian ones!

The whole matter of neo-colonialism and military intervention came to a head when France sent paratroopers and (foreign) 'legionaries' to put down the Shaba province rebellion in June 1979, only to fall out with Belgium who (having been ousted from the Congo in 1963) preferred negotiating a settlement with the rebels.

These new military imperialisms are very expensive, and the Africans are paying a high price for them. The UN Charter stresses the importance of regional arrangements for dealing with the maintenance of international peace and security. In and security. In keeping with this provision, the Charter of the OAU foresees the dangers of intra-African conflicts, so provides for peaceful settlement through an OAU Commission of Mediation, Conciliation and Arbitration. Solutions to many delicate issues have already been found through this machinery. But there is no 'news value' in settling disputes. We give too little credit to the way Africans are settling their own disputes without either Western or Soviet help. The Western news media are grossly defective about peace.

It is essential for outside Powers to keep away from the unfortunate surge of conflicts continuing in the Horn of Africa. This has already resulted in vast numbers of casualties and made a million people homeless, especially in the province of Ogaden (Ethiopia). Its long-term solution requires a peaceful settlement consistent with the principles of the Charters of both the OAU and the United Nations, not more weaponry and more US bases.

Addressing a recent meeting of the OAU in Khartoum, the UN Secretary-General Kurt Waldheim warned: 'We cannot overlook questions about outside intervention in disputes that are essentially intra-African.' Many African leaders are apprehensive lest their continent become the arena for power bloc confrontations. 'These disputes must be dealt with *inside the framework of international law*. It is only the strict observance of this rule of law, as defined by the United Nations,' he said, 'which will ensure peace and progress in Africa.'

(2) The Turks grab Cyprus

The dilemma in Cyprus is not a simple exercise of devolution of powers from an existing central government to its component parts, a compromise between the conflicting demands of two national communities. During recent history, some Greek Cypriots looked upon Cyprus as a Greek land destined to be united with Greece; while the Turkish Cypriots looked upon the island as an old Turkish land and they adamantly refused to be 'colonized' by Greece. Both these nationalistic viewpoints are irrelevant to the present need for a settlement. The problem of keeping the peace, therefore, as presented to the United Nations,

141

has been very much like Solomon's 'baby'. In fact, it is much more complicated, since the Turks now *insist* on cutting the baby in two!

Through the centuries, the two national communities have jealously guarded their national identity, while each cherished its own 'national' aspirations. So it was almost inevitable that the two communities would come into violent collision. But in 1960 the two communities accepted a compromise and worked out (when 'decolonized' by Britain) a republican constitution. The two national communities then agreed, by texts signed in London, to forgo past aims in lieu of a 'partnership Republic'. Under agreed terms of co-operation they shared the legislative, executive, judicial and other functions.

Since Greece and Turkey – both members of NATO – have quite a number of 'private' grievances to settle against each other, their open conflict in Cyprus contains volatile material indeed. Hence, the crucial importance of the UN's peacekeeping role. The function of the United Nations peacekeeping force in Cyprus (UNFICYP) was originally defined by the Security Council on 4 March 1964 as follows: 'in the interest of preserving international peace and security, to use its best efforts to prevent a recurrence of fighting and, as necessary, to contribute to the maintenance and restoration of law and order and a return to normal conditions'.

However, in 1974 the Turkish army invaded Cyprus and took over the north-eastern provinces with great savagery, expelling 200,000 Greek Cypriots. Hence, the Security Council condemned this premeditated aggression and enlarged the authority of the Force, stating 'that in existing circumstances the presence of the United Nations peace-keeping force in Cyprus is *essential* not only to help maintain quiet in the island but also to facilitate the continued search for a peaceful settlement'.

In supervising the cease-fire lines of the Cyprus National Guard and the Turkish invaders, and also the area between those lines, UNFICYP continues to prevent a recurrence of fighting by persuading both parties to refrain from violations of the cease-fire by shooting, by forward movement, or by construction of new defensive positions. UNFICYP also continues to provide security for many farmers, shepherds and other civilians of *both* communities living or working in the area bet-

142

ween the lines. As the Turks won't permit it to operate in territory under their control, UNFICYP continues to discharge its functions with regard to the security, welfare and well-being of the Greek Cypriots and also Turks living in the northern part of the island. This military occupation by the Turkish army presents a similar pattern of oppression and injustice to the Israeli occupation areas in Palestine, as we shall explain below. These cases of deliberate military occupation of someone else's territory are the most difficult cases the UN has to resolve.

Maj.-Gen. James Joseph Quinn, of Ireland, is UNFICYP's present Commander. The strength of the Force is merely 2,500 men and it is now composed of military contingents from Austria, Canada, Denmark, Finland, Ireland, Sweden and the United Kingdom, and also civilian police from Australia and Sweden. The Secretary-General continues to keep the strength of the Force under careful review. But proposals submitted to the Secretary-General by the Turkish Cypriot side have insisted on retaining a third of the island under Turkish control. Needless to add, the President of Cyprus, Spyros Kyprianou has termed them quite 'unacceptable'. Shaky Turkish governments follow each other: so the army rules! NATO is silent.

The Cypriot Government has reluctantly agreed in principle to a compromise that Cyprus become a federated yet *unified* state; but not until the borders between the two parts reflect more justly the fact that the Greek Cypriots outnumber the original Turkish population by *four to one*, and not until the bulk of the Cypriot refugees are allowed to return to their homes and shops and farms. Peacekeeping has never been more demanding than in Cyprus, yet UNFICYP cannot advertise its day-to-day successes, while it is stopping a major shooting war from *beginning* in the dangerous eastern end of the Mediterranean. And again, a *political* settlement through the UN is the only feasible solution.

(3) Does Israel prefer territory to peace?

This was how the inveterate Ben Gurion, first Prime Minister of Israel, put it just before he died: 'Israel must choose between territory and peace.' But, so far, the changing and unstable

143

political leadership of Israel has sought to shelve that crucial decision – unless driven to do so by war, as in 1973 with Egypt. Every conceivable emotional plea and dialectical argument has been used to evade or delay a decision, *on which the peace of Israel itself ultimately depends*. The single exception to this non-acceptance of the UN's repeated solutions to ensure Israel's security – at the same time providing justice for the displaced Palestinians – occurred as a result of the disastrous Yom Kippur War in 1973. Egypt then recovered some – with more to follow – of her lost territory in Sinai. It seems that only war will get back what war lost! And now Israel's open support for the so-called 'Christians' in South Lebanon may bring war with Syria.

So let us look behind the current scene from a historical perspective. Most people simply refuse to face what the Middle East conflict is all about. To 'solve' the Palestine problem, in short, would require quite a different public attitude and a fundamental shift in political policies towards what used to be the 'Holy Land', in its total Middle East setting. Western political leaders, in office for only a handful of years, have attempted no long-term solutions. They have, therefore, only supported their own national interests, based on some kind of short-term military 'balance'. It hasn't worked and never will. They think of 'defence' and 'strategy'. But that has not only failed to solve the long-term problem of peaceful settlement, either for the Jews or the Arabs; it has also produced a major escalation of the world's arms race. Israel is a pontential flash-point of World War III, and everybody knows it.

One consequence of this failure to deal with the long-term issues surrounding peace in the Middle East has been that the tiny but hopeful nation of Israel has become a garrison state, with a GNP arms budget that is the highest in the world, even though it receives approximately half of the arms export trade of the USA. Obviously, all this is wrong. It cannot last because of its inner contradictions, which prohibit any viable solution. It is a problem that can only be solved, or understood, by standing back from it. That is why the UN approach is so important.

The late Hugh Gaitskell, in his Godkin lecture at Harvard in 1957 on 'Co-existence and the United Nations', said: 'Professional politicians, when they have been in the job for any length of time, are not well fitted for really deep thinking, partly because they have no time for it and partly because the very practice of their art involves them in continual simplifications. If the expert is a man who knows more and more about less and less, the politician is a man who knows less and less about more and more.'

Our short-term political leaders in the West have ignored two crucial trends that have happened in the Middle East during the present generation, though Western historical scholarship has explained it all over and over again for those who have time to listen. Firstly, there has been the continuing revolt of the Arab peoples since the end of the *First* World War – depressed and divided after 500 years of Ottoman hegemony. This 'surge of Islam', as it has been described, has already redrawn the world's political map. Consequently, the West now faces the political, economic, and spiritual emergence of a vast Arab-Moslem nationhood stretching from the North-West Coast of Africa, across the borderlands of India and China to Indonesia.

This is the new matrix within which the peace and security of nearly 500 million people have to be determined. The USA was trapped (in more ways than one) in this new situation without knowing what it was all about. Most unfortunately and tragically of all for Israel, she was engrafted as a Western and anti-Moslem state (for reasons we need not examine here) at the most 'strategic' corner – from the point of view of military rivalry – of this immense Arab-Moslem land mass. This small Western enclave, so recently planted there by external events in Europe, can only survive as a *de facto* and *de jure* sovereign state – as Israel should – by the closest possible co-operation with the UN, which assured its birth and gave it authenticity under international law. But that essential co-operation has been consistently rejected by Israel's militant and ex-terrorist leaders, who still see themselves living in the days of David and Goliath, but equipped with cluster bombs, napalm, and KFIR fighter-bombers.

How different, however, is the picture drawn by some Western scholars, who are nonetheless ardent promoters of Israel's security and survival. Arthur Koestler, for example, in his closely researched historical survey, *The Thirteenth Tribe*, strongly defends the *right* of modern Israel to exist, as all demo-

145

cratic people do. But he points out:'That right is not based on the hypothetical origins of the Jewish people, nor on the mythological covenant of Abraham with God; it is based on international law – i.e., on the United Nations' decision in 1947 to partition Palestine, once a Turkish province, then a British Mandated Territory, into an Arab and a Jewish State.' And he concludes:

> Whatever the Israeli citizens' racial origins, and whatever illusions they entertain about them, their State exists *de jure* and *de facto*, and cannot be undone, except by genocide . . . one may add, as a matter of historical fact, that the partition of Palestine was the result of a century of peaceful Jewish immigration and pioneering effort, which provide the ethical justification for the State's legal existence.

For this reason – as we have stressed before – the peace of the Middle East and Israel's security and survival can never be assured in military victories over her neighbours, least of all by nuclear 'defence'; but by an open acceptance of the UN's role, which gives Israel its legal validity and a constitutional basis of statehood within the family of nations. The occupied territories are *not* a safeguard of Israel's integrity or security, but a menace and a curse on its existence as a lawful entity, just as they are a violation of the UN Charter, the 1949 Geneva Convention and international law.

As a partial and *ad hoc* endeavour, 'Camp David' was marked by three characteristics, which the media have tended to forget: first, that it was the Yom Kippur War that *succeeded* in winning back for the Egyptians their lost territories in Sinai; second, that it left far more difficult issues still to be resolved, namely the restitution of captured lands belonging to other Arab neighbours, Syria and Jordan – to which we can add the freedom of south Lebanon, still under indirect Israeli military control; and third, that the restoration of the Palestinians to their occupied homeland still awaits Israel's acceptance. So there has been *no settlement*. It is significant of this failed Camp David agreement that, as part of the bargain, the US is commit-ted to contribute some 3–4 billion dollars for *more* armaments – i.e. to continue the arms race! That is why a *real* peace settlement is still desperately needed and the Palestinians must be given back their ancestral lands.

Where, therefore, does there lie a measure of hope, of peace, of security? It lies, as we have said, in the only comprehensive system of world law and peacemaking that we have in existence today. The Charter of the United Nations, of which all the Arab countries and also Israel are signatories, has set down in the plainest terms the basis of that settlement. The finely balanced phrases of Resolution 242 admit of no ambiguity, except by those who are determined to thwart it. Into this chaotic picture of differing religious and rival statehoods, the UN – to whose Charter the State of Israel owes its own existence – possesses all the needed machinery of peaceful settlement to safeguard peace in the Middle East. The question is: shall we use it?

Here, then, we can summarize the most recent decisions of the UN General Assembly (December 1979) which have reaffirmed the hope, if not the surety, of peace and survival of *all* the states involved in the Arab-Israeli conflict, comprising two fundamental and essential steps:

(1) a two-stage phased withdrawal (facilitated by minor border adjustments under UN control) of the Israeli military occupation of the Arab territories overrun in 1967; and (2) a Geneva Conference, with *all* the parties represented, to define the terms and guarantees of a permanent settlement in the interests of *all* the peoples of Palestine and of the world community as well.

The UN cannot take sides in a conflict so deep and passionate as this one. Nor can its officials, whose UN offices in Jerusalem are symbolically set in an English rose garden, legacy from the pre-war days when Britain attempted from Government House to keep peace between Jews and Arabs. Palestine will always be the home of three great religions. And, in Arab Jerusalem the *Via Dolorosa* still reminds us that the victories of the Prince of Peace were not the victories of the imperial legions, but of the humble spirit which knew no enemies.

(4) USSR claims earthly satellites

What really happened at the Big Three Conference at Yalta in 1945 has been the subject of many books. Most of these downgrade both the US and UK war leaders (Roosevelt and Churchill) as simple dupes, outwitted by the wily USSR spokesman. Stalin is usually described as the arch-conspirator who got all his own way in shaping post-war Europe just as he wanted, with everything east of the Elbe included in the new Russian empire.

But there is another view which the Yalta records reveal against a longer backcloth, supported by the documents. This less popular interpretation finds Stalin the somewhat unwilling chairman (as he was) with two old-style empires sitting on each side of him – the British Empire in fast decline and the American Empire putting up big claims, especially in the Pacific. (At Yalta, the USSR agreed to declare war – as it did – on the then undefeated Japan, at Roosevelt's strong insistence.)

The United States had, by that date, already taken over much of the financial padding of the British Empire, while the African colonies were committed to early independence. So US eyes were more on Korea and Japan and on the 'containment' of China. In this game of musical chairs on each side of the chairman the records show that Europe did not get top priority. Stalin had hardly any need to put in his strong claims for an eastern buffer zone. His tanks were, in any case, on their way deep into it, amidst the welcomes of the Poles, Bulgarians and others, who were being 'liberated', in deed and in name, from five years of terrible Nazi occupation. His allies were glad he was doing so well. The cold war has over-varnished the *facts* of how the old war ended in 1944–5. But the geography has stayed put ever since.

At any rate, the division of Europe between West and East – as we view it thirty-five years later – was almost a foregone conclusion at the defeat of Germany. Re-interpretations of Yalta, i.e. what Roosevelt *ought* to have done, what Churchill *could* have done, are now beside the point. What *is* to the point is the Soviet Union's undoubted domination over the governments of Eastern Europe, all of which are creatures *not* of abstract economic or social theory, but of the chaos and confusion of the World War II aftermath, when the communists knew their minds and what they wanted. The future of Europe was *not* a big item on the Yalta agenda; *the dismemberment of Germany was*. We forget that!

The Helsinki accords finally acknowledged in 1975 the *fait accompli* in Eastern Europe. But attention has more recently been drawn to the question of human rights – which were but a minor product of the Helsinki Final Act, occupying only two sections of that long informal but precise agreement.

The Russian tanks that invaded Hungary in 1956 and Czechoslovakia in 1968 were brutal reminders that the Warsaw Pact was *real* politics and that Moscow would take no chances with dissident governments or dissident individuals. Yet it should be recalled that in neither case was a hot war threatened or likely in Europe, least of all a nuclear war. The Pentagon did not rush to defend Budapest in 1956 nor bar the Soviet tanks in the Prague Spring. So no one *then* spoke of a Third World War. Moreover, NATO, the West's guaranteed protector, had nothing at all to say. Any more than it had anything to say, or do, when Turkey invaded Cyprus in 1974. And in 1980 NATO was sidetracked by Carter's desperate effort to handle the Persian Gulf. It proved even more helpless in the Afghanistan intervention. Where is NATO today, except as a recipient of ever more nuclear weapons?

Russia's need of 'satellites' as a tangible bastion (in Soviet eyes) between NATO and WAPO, has been by this date accepted by the West as a necessary and inevitable evil. It is a brutal fact of European life: the child of the Second World War. But where the West has a special stake is in shaping its *own* policies, so as not to encourage Russian hawks to clamp down more on Eastern Europe, as they did in Hungary and Czechoslovakia. Tito died unbroken by the Soviet 'menace'. The Afghanistan invasion cannot be traded off by arms shipments to Pakistan and China or bases in Somalia. What the West needs most to do is to *relax* tensions by means of what Admiral La Rocque calls 'war avoidance' policies. President Carter had the wisdom to discover this in good time. History will accord his 1980 stand more merit than his opponents have done.

The responsibility of the Western states has been made transparently clear by those Helsinki accords, to which their signatures are appended, alongside those of the communist states. This pledge is to fulfil their *own* obligations under the Final Act, as developed later at Belgrade in 1978 and Madrid in 1980. Its clauses, covering peaceful settlement of disputes and other specific programmes of all-European co-operation, are

149

now a commitment which rules out deliberate planning of another European war, least of all a confrontation of the United States and the Soviet Union in Europe, whilst striving for the military hegemony of the Middle East and the Gulf.

The implications of the Helsinki Final Act for peace and security in Europe are slowly coming to recognition, without their human rights appeal being overlooked. For one thing, the accords eased relations between the two Germanies; for another thing they have promoted economic ties between West Germany and Poland. After two world wars *over their soil*, West Germans are ultra-sensitive to becoming a nuclear battlefield in the 1980s. So the Helsinki 'movement' is becoming something much broader in the 1980s than a sounding-board for dissidents' petitions. Hence, Herr Schmidt's bold initiative.

In May 1980 some 130 parliamentarians from the 32 countries of CSCE (the Conference on Security and Co-operation in Europe) gathered in Brussels for an Inter-Parliamentary Conference on European Security. The IPU was founded in 1889 and is a recipient of the Nobel Peace Prize. One purpose of the May meeting was to propose plans for universal détente and progress in disarmament measures in Europe in preparation for the Madrid follow-up conference of the Helsinki accords. So disarmament *in Europe* for Europe is finding new and powerful friends at last. The 'nuclear umbrella' is already in shreds.

VII
Waging Peace

The first important step to sanity is to excoriate the '1985' mentality promoted by nostalgic World War II generals and their opposite numbers in the Kremlin. General Hackett's private World War III would be run (as he admits) by 'the older men, all with experience of the Second World War'. This applies equally to the Russians, who certainly want to get rid of war – but in their own way. Fortunately, two important things have happened since they all gained their well-earned medals. The first thing is that, by 1985, three-quarters of the earth's population will have been born *after* World War II ended. Are they not entitled to a world of their own? Are they to be buried with the dead of yesterday's wars – with the errors and follies of past wars, however heroic?

The second thing is that for 40 years quite a number of really talented people on this planet have been planning peace. They belong to all nations, all creeds, all social systems. Many small wars have been stopped and more have been prevented by (as Churchill said): 'Jaw not war!' Stopping wars does not make news, however; starting wars does. Can you get *stopping* a war onto the TV screen? George Bernard Shaw did it with a play. We need more such plays. The UN records are full of conflict prevention and peaceful settlement. But who reads them? It is not NATO, as claimed by the hawks, that has kept Europe's peace for 35 years; but these quiet peacemakers behind the

151

scenes. Not least, the influence of the non-aligned leadership at the UN has a high claim to war-prevention. Western news media miss this.

We are surely intelligent enough today to surmount the barricades of fear and misunderstanding that war-oriented chauvinists of yesterday have erected between nations in the minds of their peoples – and thus to turn the tide of this growing WAR hysteria to grind the mills of hope? Mankind cannot be so self-condemned. Addressing the UN Special Session on Disarmament (then) Prime Minister Desai of India said: 'If all this power of destruction came from the human intellect, surely that intellect can create something more compassionate and benevolent.'

Nations are afflicted with the 'virile image' of themselves. They must appear in their own view strong and invincible, in order to be convincing to their adversaries. Unfortunately, they appear to other parties to be aggressive, intransigent, unyielding and unwilling. Psycho-social problems among nations have received so far very little attention or study. Yet often these are the critical factors in the achievement or non-achievement of international agreements. This applies particularly to US views of the Soviet Union, and *vice versa*. It also applies to Israel, fighting back at centuries of persecution and ostracism.

The press and other media habitually inflate this pseudo-masculinity. It is well known, for example, that sensational press coverage of football hooliganism actually *causes* some of the violent behaviour among team supporters. Dr Roger Ingham, a psychology lecturer at Southampton University, who is working on a Sports Council project to investigate football hooliganism, has said that if all newspapers stopped publishing tomorrow, football hooliganism would decline. This style of press coverage, particularly in the popular newspapers, had a big effect on events, so he told a British Psychological Society conference: 'If supporters feel they have a reputation to keep up when they visit a new town, they will do so,' he said; and a lot of supporters who do not usually carry knives took them to a particular game because *they had been told* how violent the other supporters were. So the prediction had an effect on the actual game. How much of the 'Russian threat' belongs to this kind of psychological hooliganism?

152

It is most significant that at a meeting of Defence and Foreign Ministers to start planning what was called 'a post-Afghanistan strategy for the Alliance', one of the officials said: 'We need a consensus on the long-term Soviet threat, *otherwise public opinion will not accept the necessary defense measures*, especially outside the traditional Alliance area.' (Our italics).

The maintenance of international peace and security in a disarming or potentially disarmed world depends on the evolution of effective international institutions in peacemaking and peacekeeping to provide the security which nations are unable any longer to provide for themselves. In the absence of such means, nations will fall back on the illusions that more and more terror will bring more and more peace. That is why we must go beyond merely condemning the arms merchants and their clients. We must work hard on that 'moral equivalent to war'.

The science of peace has many advocates today. A new doctrine for modern man has been gradually pushing its way between the outmoded rival antagonisms of communism and capitalism. With the help of the Third World and the non-aligned countries, working through the UN, as we have noted, the beginning of a new type of *world* democracy is slowly emerging. As US representative Mrs Benton told the UN's Special Session on Disarmament, the important thing is to bring all these new aspects to the comprehension of the ordinary citizen.

'Fundamental changes in the world often occur without being noticed,' says Nobel Peace Prize laureate Sean MacBride. And he continues: 'An instance of this has been the important change which has been taking place since the Second World War in the centre of gravity of power, *from governments to public opinion*.' Two factors have rendered this change inevitable, he states: (1) higher standards of literacy and education, which enabled public opinion to be much better informed on national and international affairs than ever before; and (2) the development of the mass media – printed and audiovisual – which has brought news, information and views instantly to the entire human race. Even people who cannot read are instantly informed of events as they take place throughout the world. (*The Times*, 21 March 1980).

Meanwhile, disarmament campaigns across the world,

research institutes and even statesmen of the smaller and medium-sized countries – especially in Canada, the Scandinavian and some Asian countries – press for urgent interim measures to block the Big Powers from destroying the planet. Here follow a few of their on-going proposals.

(1) 'Ban the Bomb!'

This cry grows ever louder among popular movements in the UK, the US and USSR. Four types of bans are *being operated now* under the United Nations disarmament machinery, but they are meeting heavy weather from the hawks. (*See Appendix (A) for details.*)

    (1) *Nuclear Test Ban*. This has been debated at the UN since 1963, but the United Kingdom, France and the United States still oppose it. Underground testing still continues; while France continues testing in the atmosphere and in the oceans, refusing to sign the 1963 Partial Test Ban Treaty. France has so badly damaged parts of the South Pacific atoll of Mururoa with its underground nuclear weapons testing that it may move the tests to another island in French Polynesia. Underground testing has enabled nuclear weapon states to develop new generations of warheads. If it were stopped *it would freeze the nuclear arms race*.

    (2) *A Moratorium*. Haven't we already enough nuclear weapons to blow up the planet six times? And more conventional weapons and men under arms than ever before in 'peacetime' in human history? Can't we call it a day and *STOP* piling on the agony? Romania put this proposal before the 1978 UN Special Session on Disarmament, and has been pressing it at the Committee on Disarmament in 1980:

> All participating states should agree to freeze military expenditure, military forces and armaments at the 1978 level, and beginning as early as 1979, to move on to their gradual reduction. In the first stage, up to 1985, the reduction should be between 10 and 15 per cent of the present levels and should cover all components of the armed forces, land, sea and air, and all categories of weapons.

154

(3) *Nuclear Free Zones*. These are beginning, but the Big Powers (or their satellites) are blocking their extension. Latin America has been declared a nuclear free zone under the 1967 Tlatelolco Treaty. But Argentine and Brazil are reneging. India presses for an Indian Ocean Nuclear Free Treaty. But Britain, US and Russia are each opposed to it. Middle Eastern Arab nations want to keep out nuclear weapons, but the superpowers refuse. In their midst, Israel clings to nuclear 'options' to safeguard her illegally occupied territories. So the struggle for sanity in the world's danger zones goes on. East of Eden Britain has nowadays most to gain, least to lose by backing the Indian Ocean Free Zone Treaty. Conversely, on what is called 'NATO's northern flank' and what the Swedes and Danes prefer to call 'the Sea of Peace', the Russians are manoeuvring six nuclear-equipped submarines in the Baltic.

(4) *Outer Space Treaty*. By this 1967 Treaty, over seventy nations prohibited the placing of nuclear weapons in orbit. But the Big Powers are now thinking up new devices for destroying satellites in orbit. However, American and Soviet officials have been wisely having preliminary talks on hunter-killer satellites in Bern recently, in order that they may develop a better understanding of each other's views. This is good news. Hunter-killer satellites would be able to destroy or capture other craft in orbit. These ambitious giants need watching. The talks will continue at a later date. We must press for their conclusion by an extension of the 1967 Treaty, which would also prohibit earth-based laser weapons.

(2) A world disarmament conference?

The convening of this Conference was pressed at the 1978 Special Session on Disarmament. Although both Russia and China and nearly all the small and medium states want it, the US and UK so far oppose it. Why? Other nations in NATO are divided: some for, some against. Where do *you* stand?

The 1978 Special Session put off a decision for four years. That means 1982 will be a critical year to prepare for. There is much to be done before that date. Crucial decisions must be taken by then. Imagine – a World Disarmament Treaty to replace the NATO and WAPO pacts! But arms and development are so tied up together that 1982 will witness a fierce struggle between the arms insisters and the war resisters. The contest will be particularly acute in the United States, for obvious reasons. And the Russians will have a field-day with propaganda. It is the Pied Pipers that call the tune; but it will be the children who will die.

Meanwhile, in the summer of 1980 another special session of the UN General Assembly will have met in New York to deal with the relations of development to disarmament. But these continuing efforts of the UN to provide a bridge between the so-called developed nations and the developing world are being frustrated by the insistence of the Big Armed Powers on putting their military strategies first.

The crude and self-defeating USSR blunder in Afghanistan in January 1980 was followed by the US' threats of widening the battle area to include the whole Middle East and Gulf region. Obviously, there must be found some spot on the planet where reason and sense can be brought to bear on this unilateral thuggery? The United Nations has been painfully and slowly building the global machinery and psychology – called 'political will' – to master the anarchy of irresponsible statesmanship. And there is now an expert committee at work on 'confidence building measures'.

In opening the second Session of the Committee on Disarmament on 5 February 1980, the Secretary-General said:

> The Committee is now called upon to initiate constructive negotiations on a number of important questions. The participation for the first time of the five nuclear-weapon states in this negotiating body should open new opportunities for concrete progress in . . . a comprehensive nuclear test ban, with its direct bearing on the halting of the arms race and the strengthening of the non-proliferation regime, nuclear disarmament, the prohibition of all chemical and radiological weapons, effective arrangements for assuring non-nuclear-weapon states against the use or threat of use of nuclear weapons – all these are subjects which need to be dealt with urgently for reducing the appalling threat to the human community.

156

The urgency of these steps becomes more strident as war fears spread across Europe – especially in West Germany, which has been twice dismembered within living memory. While, across the frontier, the Soviet Union has told France that it would *increase* nuclear arming if Western Europe deployed the 572 new weapons. This message, which accused the US of trying to 'Europeanize nuclear war while America digs in across the Atlantic,' was delivered in a speech in Paris by Soviet Ambassador Chervonenko. 'Soviet arms control specialists are telling US contacts that they are prepared to plunge into another round of the arms race, but would much rather not do so.' (*IHT*, 28 June 1980).

The US Congress would seem, over 35 years, to avoid even mentioning the UN; while refusing to ratify Human Rights Covenants, cold-shouldering ILO coventions, defaulting on financial contributions, delaying the important SALT II plans, backing the vetoing of Security Council resolutions on Israel, and ignoring UN disarmament proposals. Yet, when the US administration gets into a real jam (e.g. over Iran) two things become evident: the first is that the massive US arms build-up proves *useless* to protect US treaty rights; and the second is that President Carter has to go hat in hand to the Security Council, then to the World Court, and not least to the Secretary-General himself to go to Teheran himself, and then send a UN enquiry committee, to try to get the hostages out of the embattled US Embassy.

So why not make a habit of using the UN's unique offices in the first place – ahead of others – and so help to set up an example to build up the rule of law in this dangerous world? It is when governments and their peoples say 'it is *OUR* UN, we must use it for our security and welfare', that one of the main purposes of the Charter will be achieved. For it states (Art. 2): 'All members, in order to ensure to all of them the rights and benefits resulting from membership, shall fulfil in good faith the obligations assumed by them in accordance with the present Charter.'

This is how one American citizen (Mr Walter Hoffman, Chairman of the Campaign for UN Reform) argued in a telegram to President Carter in December 1979:

WE URGE YOU TO AVOID UNILATERAL MILITARY ACTION IN THE CURRENT IRANIAN CRISIS UNDER ALL CIRCUMSTANCES. US ARMED INTERVENTION COULD HAVE DISASTROUS CONSEQUENCES AND COULD TRIGGER WORLD WAR III. KEEP WORKING THROUGH UNITED NATIONS SYSTEM IN SPITE OF ITS WEAKNESSES. WE COMMEND YOU FOR BRINGING HOSTAGE ISSUE TO UN SECURITY COUNCIL AND TO INTERNATIONAL COURT OF JUSTICE. BLOCKADE SHOULD NOT BE IMPOSED UNLESS UN APPROVAL IS OBTAINED. URGE YOU TO ASK FOR UN OBSERVERS AND UN MEDIATION. ASK UN TO OFFER TO PROVIDE FORUM TO INVESTIGATE ALLEGATIONS AGAINST THE SHAH IN RETURN FOR RELEASE OF HOSTAGES. UN IS OUR ONLY HOPE OF BRINGING HOSTAGES BACK ALIVE AND MAINTAINING WORLD PEACE.

No one who has read thus far will doubt the magnitude of the issues facing the world in the 1980s. They will determine whether some species of Hackett game is to be played out to its logical conclusion (*sic*), or whether the switch can be made in time from Doomsday to Development. The 1970s were designated by international agreement as both the Disarmament Decade and the Development Decade. The fact is that the world community has failed in both directions. Our defence bills have increased, in real terms, at some 2.5 per cent a year through this decade, which has seen no real disarmament. In fact, the MAD race has accelerated faster than ever before, especially in developing countries. There is worse to come, unless we *STOP*!

In 1976, the UN Committee for Development Planning stated: 'Unless there can be a veritable revolution in the *political will* of the world's most favoured countries between now and 1980 . . . the Development Decade is almost sure to fail . . . The single and most massive obstacle is the worldwide expenditure on national defence activity.'

It is now accepted by economists that unless there is a reallocation of resources from defence to development, the hopes for the world's desperate call for a new international economic

158

order (NIEO) are doomed to frustration. The realization that the NIEO could succeed only if the arms race could be *reversed* and resources reallocated to development, stimulated the non-aligned countries to call for the Special Session devoted to Disarmament in 1978. For the first time in world history, the (then) 149 members of the United Nations considered where the arms race was leading them, and how it could be halted. The more important stage will come in 1982. We repeat: 'Where do *you* stand?'

If reduced to a simple denominator, this Report deals with peace. War is often thought of in terms of military conflict, or even annihilation. But there is a growing awareness that an equal danger might be chaos – as a result of mass hunger, economic disaster, environmental catastrophes, and terrorism. So we should not think only of reducing the traditional threats to peace, but also of the need for change from chaos to order. (The Brandt 'North-South' Report, 1980).

(3) Remote-sensing techniques

One of the chronic obstacles to stopping the arms race in the past has been lack of verification. What happens if a nation cheats on its promises to disarm? So disarmament agreements have been blocked in two ways. The Americans have said: 'We don't trust you; we must have our inspectors go in and see if you are doing what you agree to do.' The Russians reply: 'We don't trust you either; we won't have your inspectors prowling around our secret installations!'

This is a spurious argument at best. If a mutual bargain to cut down arms on both sides takes so much time and trouble to reach, the possibilities of its breach are remote, because both sides *want* it. The big thing is to get the cuts agreed in the first place, because obviously they will have to benefit all sides. For example, a recent State Department bulletin reads:

US participation in SALT is based not on blind trust in the USSR but upon an expectation that the Soviets will act in

159

their own best interest. It is in their interest to restrain the nuclear arms race and not to start a nuclear war that would destroy their society. Arms competition is more burdensome for them because they are the poorer country, and more dangerous because they would be at a disadvantage in an all-out race with a competitor of our strength, resources and technology.

In the UN discussions, progress has been stalled on 'on-site' inspection. Now the argument is beginning to wear thin. Because, we might say, we have raised our sights. Since the days of Gary Powers, and his notorious U2 gamble, there is probably not a nuclear weapon site in either the Soviet Union or continental Europe, or the United States, that has not been photographed – even down to details of postage stamp size. Hence, the 'other side' knows where to hit, within a couple of yards, if it can. This revolution in aeronautical science has now made nonsense of the strategists' theory that they don't know what the other side is doing, though the M-X tunnels will present (temporarily) some extra problems.

Even as far back as the Cuban crisis in 1962, US delegate Adlai Stevenson was able to screen for the information of the UN Security Council large-scale photographs of exactly where Khrushchev's missiles were installed. Since that date not a spot on the surface of the globe is hidden from the aerial spy's candid camera. What are we waiting for?

Scientists will soon put an experimental sensing device 1,500 feet under the sea floor to see if it improves earthquake monitoring, so the US National Science Foundation has announced. This seismic device will be the first ever placed permanently under the sea bottom, and could be the forerunner of a network of *neutral* instruments placed by the UN throughout the oceans of the world.

The Swedish Government told the UN Special Session in 1978 that the main part of a verification system under a comprehensive Test-Ban Treaty should consist of an international exchange of seismological data from a global network of seismological stations. Sweden is therefore participating in the on-going efforts within the framework of the Committee on Disarmament pursuing this matter in Geneva. 'The right of full

160

access by parties to a comprehensive test-ban treaty to relevant data is of vital importance', and the Government says: 'Measures should be taken also to enable States which have limited resources to make an independent assessment of globally-collected data. For this purpose an international system consisting of a network of seismological stations and international data centres will need to be established.' Sweden has backed this up by offering to establish, to operate, and to finance an international seismological data centre.

The UN's Expert Group on Seismic Detection (set up by a General Assembly vote of 124 to none) recommended in 1979 the establishment of an international control and monitoring system, consisting of a global network of some 50 seismological stations, as well as arrangements for fast worldwide exchange of data over the global system of the World Meteorological Organization (WMO). The Group called for special data centres, strategically located throughout the world, for use by participating states. The Group intends to submit in the summer of 1981 its recommendations calling for common *action* by all the states involved.

Thus the earth is becoming – overground and underground – an open book, except for the closed minds of a jingoist minority whose dogmas inherited from past wars are so remote from commonsense that no sensing device will break through their mistrust of their fellow-men or their illusions of the virtues of violence.

Dr John Cox, in *Overkill*, has put this real issue into perspective, in more senses than one:

> So the main stumbling block in the way of disarmament is simply a lack of willingness to disarm . . . Aerial photography has proved most useful and the major military powers now have very accurate knowledge of the disposition of each other's forces and weapons, missile accuracy and numbers and many other matters of considerable military importance. These spying techniques could equally well be used to verify disarmament.

Our world pool of knowledge on 'monitoring' disarmament increases from day to day. All that is lacking is the *political will*

161

to employ today's technology to advance peace and security instead of the '1985' nightmares of yesterday's generals. Peter Jankowitsch of Austria, Chairman of the Outer Space Committee, reminds us that this UN project has now entered its third decade of co-operation. 'The first two decades begin with the first signals of *Sputnik* – full of the drama which only the exploration of a new dimension of human life can bring,' he said: 'But the third decade of space co-operation might be the one in which human presence in outer space becomes a permanent feature. We really begin to push forward the frontiers of our planet.'

Among the issues now before his Committee is the comprehensive remote-sensing of the earth from space. It is true that the communist countries are a little shy of all this disturbing revelation of their alleged earthly secrets and, especially, its threat to 'national sovereignty'. But the first pioneers of space will surely get used to it, given time.

President Giscard d'Estaing has now gone further. France presented to the Special Session in 1978 specific proposals for setting up an 'international satellite monitoring agency', as a permanent organ of the United Nations. The UN satellite system, France has said, could remove some of the obstacles on the path of international safeguards and inspection for disarmament agreements. 'This satellite monitoring agency would become an essential adjunct to disarmament agreements and to measures to increase international confidence and security.' The monitoring agency 'shall be responsible for collecting, processing and disseminating information secured by means of earth observation satellites'.

Under the French plan any state that has a complaint about a violation of an agreement to which it is a party could apply to the monitoring agency. The plan also points out that the Security Council might well take action by invoking Article 34 of the United Nations Charter which authorizes it to 'investigate any dispute or any situation which might lead to international friction or give rise to a dispute'. France again pressed this plan at the Committee on Disarmament in March 1980. France's proposal for an all-*European* Disarmament Treaty we take up later.

Proposals from other countries come crowding in. There is no

162

longer any excuse for the Big Nuclear Powers to hide their silos, their troop movements, their storage depots – *because they can't*. There is no longer any possibility for either Americans or Russians to shield behind secrets hidden in tunnels! A new era has begun. The Outer Space Treaty of 1967, which over 70 nations have signed, can now be effectively enlarged and equipped with the International Satellite Verification Agency, in fulfilment of Article III, which reads: 'States Parties to the Treaty shall carry on activities in the exploration and use of outer space . . . in accordance with international law . . . in the interest of maintaining international peace and security and promoting international co-operation and understanding.'

VIII
Peace Soldiers Arrive

At 4 o'clock in the morning of 4 November 1956, the Canadian representative, the Hon. Lester Pearson, introduced into the General Assembly debate that had been going on heatedly all the previous day and night, a proposal to send a contingent of 'neutral' soldiers, selected from some half-dozen smaller states, to stand between the Israelis and the Egyptians who were then fighting as a result of Israel's aggression in Sinai, backed by the British and French Governments. Thus, UNEF (UN Emergency Force) was born. It was actually a child of Dag Hammarskjold's brain, for he planned its 'modalities'. And it stayed in position as a go-between along the Israeli-Egyptian border of Gaza and Sinai for eleven years, until the fateful day on 4 June 1967 when peace was broken again and another Arab-Israel war had begun.

These remarkable UN-controlled 'police' forces, selected from friendly nations, have now been in operation – as we have seen in earlier chapters – for a quarter of a century. They have been peacekeepers in Kashmir, Cyprus, Congo, Syria and Egypt, and now in Lebanon. Their role has not always been a simple or easy one and they have thus far been assembled on an *ad hoc* basis. But, in that quarter of a century, techniques have been improvised and developed, political obstacles have been overcome, and finances have been provided by the UN Security Council. Thus, the world community has gained a new and

164

flexible instrument to fight the peace-breakers and the war-mongers. So the UN peace-keepers are here to stay.

This is only a beginning. Many proposals are on foot to develop UN-peacekeeping operations into an effective and *permanent stand-by policing system* to outwit and, one day, replace the militarists altogether.

Such UN peace-keepers differ *fundamentally* from national military forces, though for the time being they are being drawn from them. Here is a capsule list of some of the ways in which they must be differentiated from national armies:

(1) They are servants of the world.

(2) They do not take sides in an armed struggle.

(3) They are selected from national forces having no direct interest in the conflict.

(4) They 'police' the local situation, while the Security Council decides on the *political* issues involved.

(5) They serve under a UN Commander, who is responsible to the Secretary-General.

(6) They must not shoot or use military weapons, except when under attack and in self-defence.

(7) They are selected and especially trained in techniques to anticipate and prevent local violence.

(8) They come at the invitation of the country concerned, not as an 'occupation' army.

(1) Policing the Middle East

No one assumes that this crucial experiment in peace-keeping is without blemishes. Some governments that prefer their own orthodox methods of military force have obstructed or opposed the UN peace-keeping operations, or they have refused to allocate material or men or finances to support it. Nonetheless, this dramatic challenge to the hoary war system of past ages has already marked up some valuable achievements during the last dozen or so years. The following three specific examples are taken from the Middle East alone, and they are likely to continue until the Israeli leaders decide to fulfil their obligations under the UN Charter and international law.

(1) *Egypt*. Following the Yom Kippur War in 1973 a UN

agreement called for the establishment of an *ad hoc* UNEF-manned buffer zone separating Israeli and Egyptian security zones, in which armaments would be limited. The disengagement required the withdrawal of Israeli forces holding territory west of the Canal. At Kilometre 101, the parties agreed on 24 January 1974 on plans for the successive phases of disengagement and a time-table for redeployment by the military forces on the two sides.

The Chiefs of Staff of Israel and Egypt signed a map entitled 'Plan of separation of forces'. General Ensio Siilasvuo, the former UNEF Commander, who chaired the meetings, also signed the map. 'Thus, we have successfully concluded these meetings at Kilometre 101,' he declared: 'I would hope that history may record one day that the initial step towards understanding, reconciliation and peace in the Middle East began here at Kilometre 101.'

Under the UN plan, UNEF positioned itself in temporary buffer zones whose locations would shift as the process went on. There was also a 'buffer time' of UNEF control, following Israeli withdrawal and prior to the arrival of Egyptian forces. From the time the process began, the military situation remained quiet. There were 6,000 UNEF troops involved. Meantime, successive Security Council and General Assembly resolutions since 1974 have insisted – but in vain – that Israel gets completely off Egyptian soil (including Gaza). Had this been done *there would have been no need for 'Camp David'* and all the confusions that followed. Poor Carter was caught between the Devil and the Deep Blue Sea.

(2) *Sinai*. In addition to the original UNEF presence in Sinai, the United States (playing a painful but mediatory role between Israelis and Egyptians) worked out an 'early warning' system to ensure that military outposts would not become military strong points. The US also contributed $10 million in equipment to help the UN hold this line firm, all the way south from Gaza to Suez. Besides a tactical early warning capability of some hours, the sensors could detect vehicle movements up to 15 kilometres through electronic sensors – optics during the day and infra-red at night. The total system, if developed for later contingencies, has also a 'strategic' early warning capability. An analogous operation on the Golan Heights continues and is limited to aer-

ial photo surveillance. One day this same system will be applied to *prevent* wars, by being set at danger spots. The UN marches silently on!

(3) *Lebanon*. The most speedy UN peace-keeping mission to date was mounted within 48 hours of Israel's lightning invasion of South Lebanon on 15 March 1978. The Security Council had called an emergency meeting and passed *unanimously* Resolution 425 demanding Israel's immediate and complete withdrawal. It also provided for the handing over of the occupied territory to the care of UNIFIL (UN Interim Force in Lebanon) on behalf of the sovereign Lebanese Government. It was believed that Israel had intended to hold on to the captured territory, as yet another 'buffer' against PLO attacks. *UNIFIL received clear guarantees from the PLO not to return to the southern frontier.*

Israel was finally pressured by the Western powers to leave Lebanon after a 91-day occupation. Instead of handing over control to UNIFIL, however, which then had 6,000 troops under the command of Major-General E. A. Erskine of Ghana, Israel attempted to block the UN from entering the designated border zones. Israel pursued its own military policy in opposition to the UN by transferring the territories it had overrun to a 'Christian' rebel army of about 500 irregulars, supported and equipped by Israel. Not unnaturally, the PLO withdrew their guarantee to leave Northern Israel alone, and the raids recommenced. The Lebanese delegate at the UN, Ambassador Tueni, pleaded with the Security Council for help in defending Lebanese sovereignty, made precarious by both PLO and Israel's front men, as well as Syrian incursions after a savage two-year civil war.

But for UNIFIL's skilful strategy, as directed by the Security Council, Lebanon would have been split and dismembered by these three outside aggressors. This story has been all too soon forgotten or never known. Approximately 6,000 troops from nine United Nations members (Canada, Fiji, France, Iran, Ireland, Nepal, Nigeria, Norway and Senegal) still remain on extremely delicate service, effectively denying infiltration by Palestinians with a combination of persuasion and coercion. At the same time they have tried to confine the Israeli-armed so-called 'Christian' militia in Israeli uniforms, to a local nuisance

167

value. But Major Haddad, a rebel-traitor to his own country, Lebanon, maintains his private army of some 500 rebel soldiers in a six-mile wide enclave on the Israeli-Lebanon border, financed and controlled by the Israeli Government, in defiance of UN decisions and the decent opinion of mankind.

Nonetheless, thanks to the presence of UNIFIL, half a million Lebanese have been given, for the first time in many years, security of the kind which enables crops to be harvested, children to attend school, villagers to meet without fear. One of the first Lebanese children born in the South after the UN-peace-keeping force took the matter in hand was gratefully named Unifil.

Once again this is a holding action, until the Geneva Conference of all parties meets to restore the Palestinians to their own territory and effect a just and definitive settlement of the Arab-Israeli conflict. That this possibility is coming closer today was evidenced by Mr Arafat's positive reaction to a statement by the former chief of Israeli military intelligence, General Yehoshafat Harkabi, a reformed hawk, who supports the 'Peace Now' movement, and who declared: 'I am for finalizing the conflict, but you can't do that without recognizing that the Palestinians, like any other human group, deserve self-determination. I am for a Palestinian State.' (*Herald Tribune*, 7 May 1980).

(2) Peace training for the 1980s

A great deal has been written in recent years about the possibility of reducing violence – i.e. war – between states. Our previous chapters have shown that we are on the edge of new techniques, new remedies for overcoming violence and war. But we have a long way to go yet. Most people – statesmen, generals, journalists, the common man – are not ready for it. It is this lack of knowledge, this failure to understand how *international* violence between sovereign states can be transformed into an ordered peace, that keeps this cruel and absurd arms race going at full tilt. But peace organizations and peace research institutes (*see names in Appendix (B)*) are multiplying as the war danger grows more ominous.

Let us review, in brief, what some writers have been saying about this. Dr Albert Einstein, shortly before his death, was quite clear about it: 'So long as security is sought through national armament, no country is likely to renounce any weapon that seems to promise it victory in the event of war. In my opinion, security can be attained only by renouncing all national military defence.'

With the founding of the United Nations, a new world order began quickly to emerge. Theory began to be put into hard practice. In *Foundation of Peace and Freedom* (1975) Antony C. Gilpin described his active part in the vast UN peace-keeping operations in the Congo during the chaos and tribal violence erupting over the Katanga conflict of the 1960s. He writes:

In practice, the first task of the UN Forces was to restore law and order and thus remove any excuse for Belgium to retain troops in the Congo . . . These developments brought the UN face to face with the internal political problems of the Congo, a situation made even more difficult some two months later by the split that occurred between President Kasavubu and Prime Minister Lumumba, followed by the seizure of power by the then Colonel Mobutu.

The heavy responsibility the UN administration undertook in stabilizing the Congo nation (Zaire) – in which operation Dag Hammarskjold met his death – brought the UN intervention a step forward from merely holding the line, as in Sinai or Cyprus, or now Lebanon, to an all-round re-establishment and administration of an immense African territory, which other-wise could have led to an internecine African war.

The *peaceful* transition of Namibia, following similar lines to the successful Zimbabwe example – from colonization to inde-pendence and from South Africa's *apartheid* to multi-racial nationhood – is a further extension into the 1980s of 'preventa-tive peacekeeping' under UN Charter principles, assisted by the West's comprehension and co-operation. Mr Evan Luard, then Under-Secretary for Foreign and Commonwealth Affairs, drew attention to this process, as reported in the House of Commons on 8 June 1978:

Improvements in the availability of United Nations forces was not enough. Peacekeeping forces were mobilized only after peace had broken down ... it was necessary for the United Nations to be in a position to use its influence earlier, to try to prevent such situations arising in the first place. The Organisation needed to improve its capacity for crisis anticipation.

That meant having the capability of keeping all possible crisis areas under regular review, he said, so that action could be taken by the Organisation to reduce tension in the area or to promote a settlement *before* a stage of fighting had begun. It was necessary that the Security Council should have at its disposal techniques that would enable it to go to the root of the problem and promote a settlement of a dispute among the parties.

Hence, more and more attention is being given today to the selection and training of peace-makers and peace-keepers. One of these organizations, the International Peace Academy, directed by General Indar Rikhye, one-time military adviser to the Secretary-General, operates on the basis that 'UN peacekeeping is essential to any future settlement' – anywhere in the world. General Rikhye says:

Peacemaking is defined as the process of using all peaceful means to resolve conflicts. This may require direct and bilateral negotiations or the mobilisation of regional and multinational institutions in support of such efforts. But ... since peace-building encompasses the entire environment of mankind and is best left to the expertise of the social scientists, the International Peace Academy has devoted its primary attention to the study of peacekeeping and peacemaking.

The Academy designs and conducts professional international training seminars for diplomats, military officers, academicians, and policy-makers in the subjects of peacekeeping, mediation and negotiation. It also produces publications and teaching materials of immediate practical use by professionals in governments, and teachers at institutes of higher education, both national and private.

170

Just how revolutionary this training has to be is shown by one of the Academy's expert advisers. Brigadier Michael Harbottle, former chief of staff in Cyprus, sums it up in his *The Blue Berets* (1971) as follows:

It might be hard to believe that without the authority of a rifle a soldier can achieve very much in the way of peace-keeping, when the contestants are so obviously anxious to get at each other's throats; but he can and he does. The rifle he carries provides him with his means of self-protection, not a passport for violence ... Peacekeeping is an impartial act and impartiality in this context means non-alignment with either side in a dispute, ideally to the extent of total detachment from the controversial issues at stake.

(3) Education for disarmament

But peace soldiering goes far beyond the work of professionals on the spot; it goes into the homes of the common people, into their work places, and into their schools. The importance of public education in stopping the arms race must by now be clear. There are many obstacles to the realization of disarmament and the establishment of a new order of mutual respect and toleration between nations of different histories and social systems. Obsolete ways of thinking *must* be changed if these objectives are to be achieved.

Unfortunately, many people are not prepared to accept the practical consequences of peacemaking. Transforming such mental attitudes on how these problems fit together in a global perspective will require an immense effort in all educational and information fields. The very imbecility of the arms race has forced us to look at the world differently from even a generation ago. The implications of peace and security for the common man must be shown in this new light. Education and information thus have a crucial role in training *all* people to live together as modern societies in One World.

In developing school education about security through disarmament, the difficulties will be complicated by special techni-

171

cal problems. Curricula and syllabuses must be opened up to accommodate new subject-matter. Suitable teaching in this field will require special preparation and the mastering of new bodies of information, as well as adapting teaching approaches to new purposes.

Education aimed at developing a loyalty to the principles of peace and disarmament cannot, however, be a purely cognitive process. It must also have an effective moral impact, which cannot be achieved simply by transmitting information. The school should be a place where a mature attitude towards a warless world should *begin*.

At the university level, a central problem is to develop coherent programmes of teaching the principles and techniques of peace. Specialized courses on the subject, although increasingly offered, are still very rare. The part played by universities, however, in producing community leaders and shaping the intellectual character of society makes it particularly urgent that they should present programmes broad enough to reach all students, regardless of their specialization.

The moral and intellectual, as well as the economic struggle of the 1980s is essentially between the arms race and the human race. How long this struggle will take, we do not know. We do know something of the perils of continuing as we are, a planet of divided and hostile sovereign states.

Happily, for our generation, a whole new range of global institutions is arising, within and around the United Nations family of organizations, which are laying the foundations of a new world order. All this is rendering the phobia for more and more weapons yet more irrelevant and ridiculous as each new institution comes into focus.

One of these global institutions is UNESCO. At a consultation in Paris in January 1980, attended by several hundred educators from across the world on the subject 'Education for Disarmament', Mr Frank Field, from the World Federation of UN Associations, with branches in some 55 countries, said:

Education for peace and for disarmament is based on the belief that if attitudes can be changed, wars can be prevented, or at least the chances of armed conflict greatly reduced. The Constitution of UNESCO (1946) states that 'since wars begin

172

in the minds of men, it is in the minds of men that the defences of peace must be constructed'.

His words imply two things: (1) that decisions to make war are made by particular leaders of governments and (2) that the causes of war are to be found in the opinions and behaviour of the great mass of ordinary citizens. In the first case, it will be the *attitudes of leaders* which must be changed by the education of our ruling élites. In the other case, education takes on a much wider perspective and must be aimed at all who directly or indirectly influence decision-makers. In short, large numbers of people will be involved. But is this surprising? If the 'masses' are involved in war, obviously they must be involved in peace.

Historically, power has been the accepted basis on which international relations have been conducted. War was *accepted* as a 'continuation of diplomacy by other means'. Military conflict was deplored, but taken for granted in the society of nations, *because it posed no threats to its continuance*. Until the advent of large conscript armies in the nineteenth century, the numbers killed in a war were small, less than a fraction of those dying annually of disease. But in 1945, all that changed. The first atomic bomb killed far more people than all the Nazi air raids on the United Kingdom throughout the Second World War. A nuclear war, as we have seen, would kill in the first 'strike' between 200 and 300 million people. The basic nature of war – the ultimate end of power – has therefore changed to the point when it threatens the very existence of all our societies. That is where education for peace and disarmament must begin.

Since its establishment in 1946, UNESCO has undertaken a vast amount of research on education for peace. It has become a global storehouse of experience and information on the education of the world's citizens. Education for Peace includes a wide range of objectives, such as the development of attitudes of co-operation and universal solidarity, coupled with a determination that *international disputes should be settled without resort to armed conflict*.

Education for Disarmament is part of this larger issue of understanding the arms race and the contemporary efforts to halt it. Its subject-matter consists not only of details of

173

weaponry, military expenditures, and arms negotiations, as we outlined earlier in this book; but campaigning on specific issues such as SALT, Nuclear Proliferation, a Comprehensive Test Ban Treaty, Peacekeeping Operations, and General and Complete Disarmament; and above all, campaigning for a New International Economic Order (NIEO) as a means towards the Third World's peace and prosperity.

We therefore must seek education for disarmament in schools, beginning at the secondary level, as part of Education for Peace, and in colleges of teacher education, universities and other educational institutions, *including military staff colleges*. In primary schools the main emphasis should be on Education for Peace, though some preliminary mention might be made of the menace of the arms race. On the secondary level and in a wide range of non-governmental organizations, as well as in the mass media, disarmament education would have a far greater effect if it were presented deliberately and treated as a subject of immense public importance *in its own right*.

Finally, it should be recalled that a war planned and carried on with the weapons of mass murder raises questions not only of legality in the formal sense, but basic moral questions of a deeply personal character that every individual must answer for himself alone. As long ago as 1975, the General Assembly received from the Human Rights Commission a recommendation for the fulfilling (as it stated) of youth's 'hope and aspirations for bringing about universal peace'. It included the following appeal from youth organizations in 27 countries: 'not to conscript arbitrarily any youth to join the armed forces of his country, if such youth conscientiously objects to being involved in war'. In support of this appeal the hundreds of sponsoring youth organizations contended:

Young people who opt out of all modern war because of the possibility of the nuclear cremation of millions of human beings are often treated punitively. The willingness to recognize the objector only to colonial wars and wars of aggression harks back to the ancient tradition of the just war. It is a tenable assumption, however, that *no war can be just in the nuclear age* when a just cause can be vitiated by anti-human and genocidal weaponry.

174

The petitioners also argued that, in 'just war' thinking, it is the nation that decides if its own cause is just; but no nation, according to its own account, ever conscripts soldiers to fight anything but a just war! 'Thus, the decision to serve or to object can only rest with the human being called upon to take part in military service or war. Young people know that it is their obedience that has been, and might again be, abused in carrying out the anti-human excesses that accompany modern war.'

How appropriate, then, was the unprompted response of Anawara Khan, a little girl aged 15, of Dacca, Bangladesh, who replied thus to the test question: 'MY WORLD IN THE YEAR 2000', which was posed by the International Year of the Child campaign:

In the Year 2000 I would be 38 (*sic*). There is every possibility that I may not be still alive. But if I am, I will be an architect. I want to build buildings which will not only beautify the world but bring happiness. People who live in my buildings cannot help but smile and be happy.

Finally, I aspire that in the Year AD 2000 there will be one nation, and that is human beings; that there is one race and that is the human race; and that there is one religion and that is humanity; that there is one country and that is the earth; and lastly, that the entire mankind may lead a harmonious life of peaceful existence and tolerance.

Conclusion
Organizing for Survival

How can YOU play a part in rescuing your civilization from the perils of this runaway arms race? That is the question that remains. There is no easy answer to it, as the foregoing chapters must have revealed. But there is a mounting public consciousness and collective activity to push the warmongers back to the Dark Ages where they belong. So we conclude by citing, briefly, some of the plans of those leaders of thought who are pressing for a worldwide campaign to defeat the arms race and those who are promoting it. And we can add one or two instances of actions by groups and organizations who are already mobilizing their members to win the greatest battle of this fast-receding century – the battle of peace and security through disarmament and development.

There are certain requisites which have found a place in the foregoing pages that have been demonstrated over and over again during the last 35 years. They include these three:

(1) full use must be made of the developing United Nations system, without which all General and Complete Disarmament becomes meaningless;

(2) decisions and proposals already agreed at the UN (see the outline of some of these in Appendix (A)) must be followed through by decisions at the *national* level to implement them;

(3) the 20th century contest between capitalism (USA) and communism (USSR) must be diverted from a military confrontation to commonsense co-operation via the UN and other global mechanisms. 'Conversion capability' applies to both.

This immense effort is something quite new in global history. But the initiative for it *must* come from the West, since the UN is itself the West's own political and legal contribution and its deliberately chosen structure for solving world problems. We can't wait for the Russians to change; but we can show them how it can be done by changing ourselves.

Disarmament must be conceived today not as a negative act but in terms of *preventive* politics. We have preventive health care for the individual. Why not preventive politics of disarmament for the wellbeing of the human race? Here are some broad axioms to guide the burgeoning present campaigns:

(1) National security advances as international disarmament advances;

(2) Alternative programmes for arms reduction have to be built stage by stage, nationally and globally;

(3) The Security Council, charged with world security questions, should be resorted to habitually to *prevent* wars;

(4) The UN's ample and flexible machinery of peace settlement of disputes must become the normal centre for dealing with each crisis as it arises;

(5) The UN's peacekeeping forces must be equipped and financed by the world's governments along the lines repeatedly proposed by independent peacekeeping experts and practitioners;

(6) The continuous relationship existing between the UN system of security and disarmament and its peacemaking and peacekeeping procedures, on the one hand, and the world's sovereign governments, on the other hand, must be implemented as agreed at the 1978 Special Session, and strengthened on every level of co-operation with the non-governmental organizations as indicated below.

The World Disarmament Campaign

The World Disarmament Campaign, launched at a convention in London on 12 April 1980, accepted as its policy basis the decisions made at the Special Assembly in 1978; representatives of forty nations, now forming the UN Committee on Disarmament in Geneva (including all the nuclear powers) have been mandated by the General Assembly to carry those 1978 decisions further, by:

(1) recommending practical measures to abolish all armed forces, *except those needed for internal security* and a UN Peacekeeping Force, and

(2) preparing proposals for the reduction of armaments, leading to General and Complete Disarmament.

All governments pledged themselves openly in 1978 to co-operate in seeking disarmament along these drastic lines. The British Government gained the support of fifteen nations in submitting supporting proposals; President Carter has since called for the reduction of nuclear arms to *zero*, after SALT II is ratified; and President Brezhnev has repeated his long-advocated plea for the destruction of all weapons of mass destruction. But these clear statements by governments will not be fulfilled unless there is considerable pressure from peoples. International disarmament goals have therefore been set.

We, therefore, call on all peoples [say the organizers of the Campaign] to unite in a world-wide campaign to achieve these goals.

The Programme of action in Britain is now proceeding as follows:

(1) The participation of all sections of the community, including the Churches, Trade Unions, Political Parties, Peace Organisations, Universities, the Arts, Professions, Women, Youth, and the Trades Union Congress (as already approved by the latter's 1979 Congress).

(2) Enrolment of Sponsors, including MPs, Peers, Ministers of Religion, Councillors, Academics and representatives of other sections of the community.

(3) Formation of Local Councils in every locality to carry on the Campaign by meetings, marches, letters to the Press, and other constitutional means, such as deputations to the Government, Political Parties, Members of Parliament, and Managements of National Authorities, including the Media, Television and Radio.

(4) A National Convention to plan expanding action in preparation for the renewed UN Special Assembly in 1982; and an international meeting of Parliamentary representatives to plan united action for disarmament, as proposed by Deputies in France and Japan, together with the national disarmament movements in many other countries, thus to initiate a co-ordinated Campaign on a world-wide scale.

(5) The organization of an international petition or ballot, incorporating many millions of signatures, urging the adoption of measures outlawing weapons of mass destruction, the ending of the arms trade, and phased progress towards complete disarmament, as well as the utilization of the present expenditure on armaments for alternative employment and to bridge the global gulf between riches and poverty.

Smaller countries must lead

But why cannot these burgeoning *voluntary* movements, such as the above, look for a government's official vote somewhere, speaking for the world's conscience? Should we not seek this initiative from one or more of the Scandinavian or 'neutral' countries? For example, perhaps the Netherlands' Government might now decide to implement their significant opposition to provide bases for the 572 American nuclear missiles? The vote by the Dutch Parliament to reject the new missile plans has surely presented the Dutch Government with a unique opportunity to propose a series of phased and specific reductions, focused on the 1982 Special Session programme. Denmark, too, had not even been asked to accept missiles, after calling for a postponement of the NATO decision for six months. Norway also strongly favoured negotiating first. Here is surely fertile soil for boycotting the missile race in the 1980s?

At the same time, NATO arms control proposals do, at least, envisage talks on *limiting* Soviet SS-20 medium-range missiles and the Backfire Bomber as against limits on comparable NATO weapons in Europe. These plans could be paralleled by renewed talks in Vienna on reducing troops – especially BAOR – as well as conventional and tactical nuclear weapons in Central Europe. NATO officials have argued, of course, that the decision on deploying the new American missiles would 'strengthen the West's hand in negotiation'. So the big NATO generals would be hoisted on their own petard if smaller NATO members put forward their reduction plans as a contribution to that 'negotiation'. In any case, the deployment of the '572' could not be completed until 1983. So what are we waiting for? Time is running out for peace.

Meanwhile, the Russians do not admit that they have done anything provocative by deploying SS-20 missiles and Backfire Bombers. They point out that they *tried* to bring weapons of this sort into the SALT talks with the United States, but that the Americans objected. The Soviet Union made a concession – recognized as such by the Americans – when it went along with this. They feel that the new US weapons do, however, represent an unequal threat, for the weapons will be able to strike Soviet territory, while the SS-20 and the Backfire Bombers cannot hit the United States. Moreover, the new NATO weapons could be seen as a Western way round the SALT restrictions. So a lead by the non-nuclear powers, Netherlands and Belgium and the Scandinavians, would provide the World Disarmament Campaign with the *official* leadership that it so badly needs. The support of some 80 non-aligned nations is already assured.

Moving forward

US Arms Control and Disarmament Agency former Director, Mr William C. Foster, has said:

> Every step that helped to move us toward the control of nuclear weapons was important. Among such steps was the Test Ban Treaty of 1963. Though limited, it successfully reduced atmospheric testing and the contamination of the environment by radioactive substances. Another step of great importance was the Treaty on the Non-Proliferation of Nuclear Weapons in 1968 . . . Now in SALT II one more such opportunity presents itself . . . This is an awesome task *that we have begun*, and it is of supreme importance that we continue the effort step by step.

Until recently, public reaction to our darkening future has taken several forms. Most of it has been confined to quiet demonstrations of protest. But the signs of violent popular outrage are increasing and ominous. In Iran, for example, popular rage against bloated military programmes was a major factor in triggering revolution. The United States became the chief sufferer. But there is clearly more revulsion against the West to follow as the Pentagon's 'old boys' continue to push their dangerous hardware on other Middle East countries.

Then, throughout Western Europe, in Australia, and Canada, as well as the US, there have been large-scale demonstrations against nuclear sites and facilities. Weapons sales bazaars have received adverse public notice for the first time, and were picketed. In May 1979, Washington witnessed its largest mass demonstration since the Vietnam War, as 90,000 people marched against nuclear power *and* nuclear weapons. Also in 1979 there was initiated a new citizen development in the coalition of church, peace, and women's groups with environmentalists, scientists, and labour unions. This could be the start of the first serious public challenge to the arms race in many years, allied to the new World Disarmament Campaign inaugurated in London under the Chairmanship of Lord Gardiner, former Lord Chancellor, supported by Lord Noel-Baker and other Nobel Prize winners.

This *moral* revolt against the more-arms advocates is finding its voice at last in some unusual places across the earth. No one can stop it. For example, at what was termed the greatest Christian demonstration in the history of Fiji, attended by the Governor-General of Fiji and broadcast throughout the Pacific area, over 30,000 people gathered together to hear Dr Alan Walker of the World Methodist Council say: 'Humanity is only a push-button away from atomic weapons killing millions and destroying the centres of the world's life'. He went on: 'Irreligion is steadily destroying the Western world. Without faith in God, respect for human life, moral standards, family life and ideals of service are undermined . . . "Feed the hungry, set the poverty-captives free", is the call of the new decade.' And Dr Walker added: 'A new world economic order must be found. The present world order is collapsing. We call for the launching of a vast crusade against poverty, not for charity or aid, but for justice.'

If this was a Protestant plea from the other side of the planet,

181

it shared the same moral urgency as Pope John Paul's courageous and piercing words when visiting the NATO Defence College in 1979: 'Sensitivity to the immense needs of humanity brings with it a spontaneous rejection of the arms race, which is incompatible with the all-out struggle against hunger, sickness, under-development and illiteracy.'

A further chance on the governmental level exists at the next Conference on Security and Co-operation in Europe (CSCE), meeting in Madrid in November 1980. This time, 'security' acquires a new emphasis. Confidence-building measures and invitations to observers to watch manoeuvres have worked well, as mentioned above, since the 1975 Helsinki agreements and have reduced the chances of miscalculation and surprise attack between NATO and WAPO. The CSCE, founded in Helsinki as a *permanent* European organization, includes *all* the European states (except Albania), plus the United States and Canada – a total of 35 signatories.

The French, for instance, are fairly confident that, from the way the Russians have been publicizing their own schemes for 'a European military détente', the time has come to develop a *European Disarmament Conference*. This French disarmament plan has two phases. The first spreads the scope of reporting measures as far back as the Urals. The second phase relates to actual cuts in armaments. Such ideas are now being fitted into the proposed 1980 Madrid scheme.

There is also ample evidence, reinforced by a recent Warsaw Pact Foreign Ministers' meeting in East Berlin, of a Romanian and Yugoslav lead in a Russian arms limitation campaign. The French think that the same kind of human rights emphasis that the West placed on the Russians at Helsinki could be repeated in Madrid, if balanced by Western arms reductions that the Russians clearly want. Some NATO allies, especially the West Germans, are in favour of the French approach, on the understanding that the Alliance links security to human rights. Thus, CSCE might eventually come *to replace NATO and WAPO by an All-European Security System*. Why not?

It is not possible in a book of this kind, dealing with the arms race, to present a full blueprint of a viable world peace system,

182

other than by sketching a few sample guidelines, as we have attempted to do in these recent chapters. But all men and women of faith and good-will must acknowledge our primary need, in the declining years of this Century of Anxiety, to seek and encourage more sensible co-existence patterns between the rival imperialisms of Russia and America, which are the tap-root of the arms race.

The 35 brief years that have been misspent in pursuing this criminal exercise in military suicide is only a tiny segment of man's long existence on this planet. During the three million years or more that have elapsed since *homo sapiens* emerged from his animal ancestry as the crown of God's creation, more than one 'crisis' has threatened his race with extinction. It cannot be beyond the wit of the leaders of this generation to range themselves and their peoples on the side of life.

Appendix (A)
A Short History of Arms Pacts*

Arms reduction agreements concluded in the post-World War II period have had the following ostensible objectives: (1) prevention of the militarization, or military nuclearization, of certain areas or environments; (2) freeze or limitation on the numbers and characteristics of nuclear delivery vehicles; (3) restrictions on weapon tests; (4) prevention of the spread of specified weapons among nations; (5) prohibition of the production as well as elimination of stocks of certain types of weapons; (6) prohibition of certain methods of warfare; (7) reduction of the risk of an accidental outbreak of nuclear war; (8) observance of the rules of conduct in war; (9) notification of certain military activities; and (10) verification of obligations contracted under previously signed treaties.

The 1959 Antarctic Treaty has declared that Antarctica shall be used exclusively for peaceful purposes. It is an important demilitarization measure. But it will be in constant jeopardy so long as the question of territorial sovereignty in Antarctica has not been definitely resolved. (Signed: 1 December 1959;

*Josef Goldblat, *Arms Control: A Survey and Appraisal of Multilateral Agreements*, SIPRI, 1978 entered into force: 23 June 1961. Number of parties as of 31 December 1978: 19.)

The 1963 Partial Test Ban Treaty has banned nuclear weapon tests in the atmosphere, in outer space and under water. It has helped to curb radioactive pollution caused by nuclear explosions. But continued testing underground has made it possible for the nuclear weapon parties to the Treaty to develop new generations of nuclear warheads. They have carried out more explosions since this Treaty than before it. (Signed: 5 August 1963; entered into force: 10 October 1963. Number of parties as of 31 December 1978: 109.)

The 1967 Outer Space Treaty has prohibited the placing of nuclear or other weapons of mass destruction in orbit around the Earth and also established that celestial bodies are to be used exclusively for peaceful purposes. But weapons of mass-destruction in outer space present apparently insurmountable problems of maintenance, command and control, making it easy for the nuclear-weapon powers to forgo them. Moreover, outer space has remained open for ballistic missiles carrying nuclear weapons; and the deployment in outer space of weapons not capable of mass-destruction is subject to no restrictions. The major powers are also engaged in developing devices capable of destroying satellites in orbit, adding a new dimension to the arms race. (Signed: 27 January 1967; entered into force: 10 October 1967. Number of parties as of 31 December 1978: 78.)

The 1967 Treaty of Tlatelolco prohibits nuclear weapons in Latin America. It has established the first nuclear-weapon-free zone in a populated region of the world. But it will not achieve its principal goal, until Argentina and Brazil, the only countries in the area with any nuclear potential and aspirations, are bound by its provisions. (Signed: 14 February 1967; entered into force: 22 April 1968. Number of parties as of 31 December 1978: 22.) Additional Protocols were in the course of ratification during 1979.

The 1968 Non-Proliferation Treaty prohibits the transfer of nuclear weapons by nuclear-weapon states and the acquisition of

186

such weapons by non-nuclear-weapon states. It grew out of the realization that the possession of nuclear weapons by many countries would increase the threat to world security. But it is being gradually eroded because of the inconsistent policies of the nuclear-material suppliers, the non-fulfilment of the obligations undertaken by the nuclear-weapon powers, and the lack of guarantees that nuclear weapons will not be used against non-nuclear-weapon states. (Signed: 1 July 1968; entered into force: 5 March 1970. Number of parties as of 24 March 1980: 114.)

The 1971 Sea-Bed Treaty has prohibited the emplacement of nuclear weapons on the sea-bed beyond a 12-mile zone. But because of the vulnerability of fixed devices, such emplacement is not militarily attractive. And since the Treaty permits the use of the sea-bed for facilities that service free-swimming nuclear weapon systems, it presents no obstacle to a nuclear arms race in the whole of the marine environment. (Signed: 11 February 1971; entered into force: 18 May 1972. Number of parties as of 31 December 1978: 65.)

The 1974 Threshold Test Ban Treaty has limited the size of US and Soviet nuclear-weapon test explosions to 150 kilotons. But the threshold is so high (ten times higher than the yield of the Hiroshima bomb) that the parties cannot be experiencing onerous restraint in continuing their nuclear-weapon development programmes. (Signed: 3 July 1974; *not* in force by 31 December 1977.)

The 1972 Biological Weapons Convention has prohibited biological means of warfare. But in view of their uncontrollability and unpredictability, these weapons have always been considered of little utility. On the other hand, chemical weapons, which are more predictable and which have been used on a large scale in war, are still the subject of disarmament negotiations. (Signed: 10 April 1972; entered into force: 26 March 1975. Number of parties as of 21 March 1978: 87.)

The 1972 SALT ABM Treaty has imposed limitations on US and Soviet anti-ballistic missile defences. But the type of ABMs the

Treaty deals with cannot offer meaningful resistance to the penetration of offensive missiles. The development of new ABMs continues. (Signed: 26 May 1972; entered into force: 3 October 1972.)

The 1972 SALT Interim Agreement has frozen the aggregate number of US and Soviet ballistic missile launchers. But it has not restricted the qualitative improvement of nuclear weapons – their survivability, accuracy, penetrativity and range. Moreover, the number of nuclear charges carried by each missile has been allowed to proliferate. (Signed: 26 May 1972; entered into force: 3 October 1972. Number of parties: 28.)

The 1975 Document on Confidence-building Measures contained in the Final Act of the Conference on Security and Co-operation in Europe provides for notification of major military manoeuvres in Europe. But it does not restrict these activities. Moreover, military movements, other than manoeuvres, do not have to be notified, even though transfers of combat-ready units outside their permanent garrison or base areas, especially over long distances and close to the borders of other states, may cause greater concern than manoeuvres. (Signed: 1 August 1975.)

The 1976 Peaceful Nuclear Explosions Treaty regulates the US and Soviet explosions carried out outside the nuclear-weapon test sites and therefore presumed to be for peaceful purposes. But, apart from being a complement to the 1974 Threshold Test Ban Treaty, it has no arms control value. On the contrary, in emphasizing the importance of peaceful nuclear explosions it may have had a negative impact on the policy of preventing nuclear-weapon proliferation by providing added justification and encouragement for some non-nuclear-weapon countries to plan for an indigenous development of nuclear explosives. (Signed: 28 May 1976; *not* in force by 31 December 1978.)

The 1977 Environmental Modification Convention prohibits the hostile use of techniques which could produce substantial environmental modifications. But essentially only those techniques have been forbidden which are still the subject of scientific

188

speculation and which, if proved feasible, seem hardly usable as rational weapons of war. Manipulation of the environment with techniques which are already in existence, and which can be useful in tactical military operations, has escaped proscription. (Signed: 18 May 1977; entered into force: 5 October 1978.)

The 1977 Protocols Additional to the 1949 Geneva Conventions provide for the protection of victims of international and non-international armed conflicts. They constitute a step forward in the development of the humanitarian laws of war. But they have not forbidden any specific weapon which is excessively injurious or has indiscriminate effects. (Signed: 12 December 1977; *not* in force by 31 December 1978.)

Appendix (B)
Organizations *You* Can Join

Concerned with peace and disarmament, the following list has been selected with permission from the *Peace Diary* published by Housmans, 5 Caledonian Road, London, N1, England (01-837-4473), from which address further copies of this book can be obtained.

Great Britain

Africa Bureau, 48 Grafton Way, London W1P 5LB (01-387 3182).

African National Congress of South Africa, 49 Rathbone St, London W1A 4NL (01-580 5303).

Amnesty International, British Section, 8-14 Southampton St, London WC2E 7HF (01-836 5621).

Anglican Pacifist Fellowship, St Mary's Church House, Bayswater Rd, Headington, Oxford OX3 9EY.

Anti-Apartheid Movement, 89 Charlotte St, London W1P 2DQ.

Association of World Federalists, 40 Shaftesbury Ave, London W1V 8HJ (01-969 2803).

Baha'i National Spiritual Assembly, 27 Rutland Gate, London SW7 1RD.

J. D. Bernal Peace Library, 44 Albert St, London NW1.

Bertrand Russell Peace Foundation, 45 Gamble St, Nottingham NG7 4ET.

Birmingham Peace Centre, 18 Moor St, Queensway, Birmingham B4 7UB.

British Society for Social Responsibility in Science, 9 Poland St, London W1V 3DG.

British Soviet Friendship Society, 36 St John's Square, London EC1V 4JH.

Campaign Against the Arms Trade, 5 Caledonian Rd, London N1 9DX.

Campaign for Nuclear Disarmament, 29 Gt James St, London WC1N 3EY.

Central Board for Conscientious Objectors, c/o 6 Endsleigh St, London WC1.

Christian Action, 15 Blackfriars La., London SE1.

Christian Movement for Peace, Stowford House, Bayswater Rd, Oxford OX3 95A.

Commission for International Justice and Peace, 44 Grays Inn Rd, London WC1X 8LR.

Concerns Against Nuclear Technology, 19 Cheyne Walk, London SW3.

Co-operative Women's Guild, Pioneer House, 342 Hoe St, London E17 9PX.

Council for Education in World Citizenship, 43 Russell Sq., London WC1B 5DA.

Danilo Dolci Trust, 29 Gt James St, London WC1.

Fellowship of Reconciliation, 9 Coombe Rd, New Malden, Surrey KT3 4QA.

FOR in Scotland, 53 Kelvinside Gdns, Glasgow G20 6BQ.

Friends Peace and International Relations Committee, Friends House, Euston Rd, London NW1.

Friends World Committee, London.

Greenpeace, c/o Peace Pledge Union.

International Confederation for Disarmament and Peace, London (*see* National Peace Council).

International Friendship League, 3 Creswick Rd, London W3 9HE.

International Voluntary Service, Ceresole Ho., 53 Regent Rd, Leicester LE1 6YL.

192

Labour Action for Peace, 81 Orchard Ave, Croydon CR0 7NF, Surrey.

Liaison Committee of Women's Peace Groups, 44 Albert St, London NW1 7NU.

Liberation, 313 Caledonian Rd, London N7.

Medical Association for the Prevention of War, c/o Richardson Institute, 158 N Gower St, London NW1.

Mennonite Centre (London), 14 Shepherds Hill, London N6 5AQ (01-340 8775).

Methodist Peace Fellowship, c/o FOR.

Minority Rights Group, 36 Craven St, London WC2N 5NG.

National Council for Civil Liberties and Cobden Trust, 186 Kings Cross Rd, London WC1X 9DE.

National Peace Council and United World Trust, 29 Gt James St, London WC1N 3ES.

New Internationalist, 62 High St, Wallingford, Oxford OX10 0EE.

New Left Review, 7 Carlisle St, London W1.

Northern Friends Peace Board, 30 Gledhowwood Grove, Leeds LS8 1NZ.

Nuclear Information Network, c/o Nat. Peace Council.

Overseas Development Institute, 10/11 Percy St, London W1P 0JP.

Oxfam, 274 Banbury Road, Oxford OX2 7DZ.

Pax Christi, Blackfriars Hall, Southampton Rd, London NW5.

Peace News, 5 Caledonian Rd, London N1 9DX.

Peace Pledge Union, Dick Sheppard House, 6 Endsleigh St, London WC1H 0DX.

Religious Society of Friends, Friends House, Euston Rd, London NW1 2BJ.

Richardson Institute for Conflict Research, 158 N Gower St, London NW1 2ND.

School of Peace Studies, University of Bradford, Bradford, BD7 1DP, W Yorks.

Student Christian Movement, Wick Ct, Wick, nr Bristol BS15 5RD.

Tribune, 24 St. John St., London EC1.

Unitarian and Free Christian Peace Fellowship 53 Kelvinside Gdns, Glasgow G20 6BQ.

United Nations Assoc., 3 Whitehall Ct, London, SW1A 2EL.

Voluntary Service Overseas 14 Bishops Bridge Rd, London, W2 6AA.

War on Want, 467 Caledonian Rd, London N7 9BE.

Women for World Disarmament, North Curry ,Taunton, Somerset TA3 6HL.

Women's International League for Peace and Freedom, 29 Gt James St, London WC1N 3ES.

World Development Movement, Bedford Chambers, Covent Gdn, London WC2E 8HA.

World Disarmament Campaign, 21 Rydons Lane, Old Coulsdon, Surrey, CR3 1SU.

Young Liberals Movement, 1 Whitehall Pl., London WC2.

Australia

Amnesty International, St Kilda 3182, Victoria.

Association for International Co-operation and Disarmament, PB A243, Sydney South PO, NSW 2000.

Catholic Commission for Justice and Peace, POB J124, Brickfield Hill, NSW 2000.

Congress for International Co-operation and Disarmament, 208 Lt Lonsdale St, Melbourne 3000.

Federal Pacifist Council, Box 2598, Sydney, NSW 2001.

Friends (Quaker) Centre, 631 Orrang Rd, Toorak, Melbourne 3142.

Pax Christi, 31 Carlton South, Victoria 3053.

Peace Institute, 306 Murray St, Perth, WA 6008.

Peace Pledge Union, 3 Euston Ave, Highgate, S Australia.

Transnational Co-operative, 232 Castlereagh St, Sydney, NSW 2001.

United Nations Association, 66 Turbot St, Brisbane 4001.

Women's International League, PB 35, Fairfield, Victoria 3078.

Canada

Amnesty International, POB 6033, 2101 Algonquin Ave, Ottawa, Ontario K2A 1TI.

Canadian Peace Research Institute, 25 Dundana Ave, Dundas, Ontario L9H 4E5.

Christian Movement for Peace, 24 Alexandra Blvd, Toronto M4R 1L7.

194

Fellowship of Reconciliation, 126A St Ocean Pk, Surrey, BC.

Friends (Quaker) Centre, 60 Lowther Ave, Toronto, Ontario M5R 1C7.

Project Ploughshares, School for Peace and Conflict Studies, Conrad Grebel College, Waterloo, Ontario N2L 3G6.

United Nations Association in Canada, 63 Sparks Street, Ottawa K1P 5A6, Ontario.

Voice of Women/La Voix des Femmes, 175 Carlton St, Toronto, Ontario M5A 2K3.

Women's International League 1768 West 11th Ave, Vancouver BC, V6J 2C3.

World Federalists, 46 Elgin St, Rm 32, Ottawa, Ontario K1P 5K6.

New Zealand

Anglican Pacifist Fellowship, 56a Wai-iti, Cres, Lower Hutt (Wellington 698125).

Catholic Peace Fellowship, Box 12224, Wellington.

Christian Pacifist Society, 9 Grove Rd, Kelburn, Wellington.

New Zealand Foundation for Peace Studies, PB 4110, Auckland.

Society of Friends Peace Committee, 14 Sunnynook Rd, Takapuna North, Auckland 10.

Student Christian Movement, POB 9792, Courtenay Pl., Wellington.

United Nations Association, 1011, 10 Brandon St, Wellington.

Voice of Women, 21 Ravelston St, Dunedin.

Women's International League for Peace and Freedom, 7A Queenstown Rd, Auckland 6.

United States

American Civil Liberties Union, 22 E 40th St, New York, NY 10016.

American Friends Service Committee, 1515 Cherry St, Philadelphia, Pa 19102.

Amnesty International, 2112 Broadway, Office 309, New York, NY 10023.

Baptist Peace Fellowship, 3448 Rainbow Dr., Palo Alto, Ca 94306.

Carnegie Endowment for International Peace, 345 East 46th Street, New York, NY 10017.

Catholic Peace Fellowship, 339 Lafayette St, New York, NY 10012.

Catholic Worker Movement, 36 E 1st St, New York, NY 10003.

CCCO (Draft and Military Counseling), 2016 Walnut St, Philadelphia, Pa 19103.

Center for Global Perspectives, 218 East 18th St, New York, NY 10003.

Center for Study of Armament and Disarmament, California State College, 5151 State University Dr., Los Angeles, California 90032.

Coalition for a New Foreign and Military Policy, 122 Maryland Ave, Washington DC 20002.

Conference on Peace Research in History, University of Toledo, Toledo, Ohio 43606.

Consortium Peace Research, Education and Development, Gustavus Adolphus College, St Peter, Minnesota 56082.

Episcopal Peace Fellowship, 61 Gramercy Park N, New York, NY 10010.

Fellowship of Reconciliation, Box 271, Nyack, New York, NY 10960.

Friends Committee on National Legislation, 245 Second St, NE Washington DC 20002.

Friends of the Earth, 529 Commercial St, San Francisco.

Friends Peace Committee, 1515 Cherry St, Philadelphia, Pa 19102.

Inst. for International Policy, 120 Maryland Ave, Washington DC 20002.

Jewish Peace Fellowship, Box 271, Nyack, NY 10960.

Liberation, 136 Hampshire St, Cambridge, Mass 02139.

Lutheran Peace Fellowship, 168 W 100th St, New York, NY 10025.

Mobilisation for Survival, 198 Broadway (Rm 302), New York, NY 10038.

Movement for a New Society, 4722 Baltimore Ave, Philadelphia, Pa 19143 (215 724 1464).

National Action/Research on the Military Industrial Complex, c/o AFSC, Philadelphia.

Pax Christi, c/o Peace Studies Inst., Manhattan College, Bronx, New York, NY 10471.

Peace Digest, Lamplighter La., Newington, CT 06 111.

Peace Science Society (International), 3718 Locust Walk, CR, McNeill Bldg, Univ.of Pennsylvania, Philadelphia, Pa 19174.

Progressive, 408 West Gorham St, Madison, Wis 53703.

Society for Social Responsibility in Science, 221 Rock Hill Road, Bala-Cynwyd, Pa 19004.

Swarthmore College Peace Collection, Swarthmore, Pa 19081.

Unitarian Universalist Association, Dept of Education and Social Concern, 25 Beacon St, Boston, Mass 021088.

United Farmworkers Union, Logan Ave, San Diego, Ca 92113.

United Methodist Church, Division of World Peace, 100 Maryland Ave NE, Washington DC 20002.

United Nations Assoc. 345 East 46th St, New York, NY 10017.

War Resisters' League, 339 Lafayette St, New York, NY 10012.

Women's International League for Peace and Freedom, 1213 Race St, Philadelphia, Pa 19107.

World Council of Churches, 475 Riverside Drive, New York, NY 10027.

World Federalists Assoc., 1424 16th St NW, Washington DC 20036.

World Peace News, 777 UN Plaza, 11th Floor, New York, NY 10017.

World Without War Council, 175 Fifth Ave, New York, NY 10010.

Union of Socialist Soviet Republics

Assotsiatsiya Sodeistviya Oon V SSSR, Kirovst 24, Moscow 101000.

Institute of World Economy and International Relations, Dept of Peace Research, 2 Jaroslavskaya Ulitsa, d.3 korpus 8, Moskva 1-243.

KMO-CCP, Bogdan Khmeinisky 7/8, Moskva.

Soviet Peace Committee, Ul Kropotkine 10, Moskva 634.

International Organizations

This section includes organizations which co-ordinate their national groups and those primarily international.

Amnesty International, 8-14 Southampton St, London WC2E 7HF, Gt Britain.

Baha'i International Community, 345 E 46th St, New York, NY 10017, USA.

Christian Movement for Peace, rue Louvrex, 36, 4000 Liège, Belgium.

Christian Peace Conference, Jungmannova 9, 111 21 Praha 1, Czechoslovakia.

Eirene, 545 Neuwied 1, Engerser Str. 74B, West Germany.

Friends of the Earth, 9 Poland St, London W1V 3D9, Gt Britain.

Friends World Committee for Consultation, 30 Gordon St, London WC1H 0AX, Gt Britain.

International Committee of the Red Cross, 17 Avenue de la Paix, 1211 Genève, Switzerland.

International Confederation for Disarmament and Peace, 6 Endsleigh St, London WC1H 0DX, Gt Britain.

International Court of Justice, Peace Palace, The Hague, Netherlands.

International Fellowship of Reconciliation, Hof van Sonoy, Veerstraat 1, Alkmar, Netherlands.

International League for Human Rights (HR), 777 United Nations Plaza, Suite 6F, New York, NY 10017, USA.

International Peace Academy, 777 United Nations Plaza, New York, NY 10017, USA.

International Peace Bureau, rue de Zurich 41, CH-1201 Genève, Switzerland.

International Peace Research Association, PO Box 70, 33101 Tampere 10, Finland.

International Registry of World Citizens, 55 rue Lacépède, Paris 75005, France.

International Youth and Student Movement for the United Nations, 5 Chemin des Iris, 1216 Cointrin Genève, Switzerland.

Pax Christi International, PO Box 85627, NL-2040, Den Haag, Celebesstr 60, Netherlands.

Pax Romana, 1 route de Jura, PB 1062, CH-1701 Fribourg, Switzerland.

Servas International, 268 W 12th St, New York, NY 10014, USA.

Service Civil International, 35 ave Gaston Diderich, Luxembourg.

198

Transnational Institute, Paulus Potterstr, Amsterdam, Netherlands.

United Nations, New York, NY 10017, USA. *Sec-Gen* Kurt Waldheim.

Educational, Scientific and Cultural Organisation, Place de Fontenoy, 75700 Paris, France.

International Labour Organisation, 4 route des Morillons, CH1211 Genève 22, Switzerland.

War Resisters' International, 35 rue van Elewyck, 1050 Bruxelles, Belgium.

Women's International League for Peace and Freedom, 1 rue de Varembé, 1211 Genève 20, Switzerland.

World Conference of Religion for Peace, 777 United Nations Plaza, New York, NY 10017, USA.

World Council of Churches, 150 route de Ferney, 1211 Genève 20, Switzerland.

World Assoc. of World Federalists and World Federalist Youth, Leliegracht 21, Amsterdam C, Netherlands.

World Federation of Scientific Workers, 40 Goodge St, London W1P 1FH, Gt Britain.

World Federation of United Nations Associations, Palais des Nations, 1202 Genève, Switzerland.

World Peace Council, Lönnrethinkatu, 25 Helsinki 18, Finland.

World Peace Through Law Centre, 400 Hill Bldgs, Washington DC 20006, USA.

World Student Christian Federation, 37 Quai Wilson, 1201 Genève, Switzerland.

Further Reading

Books on Disarmament, and those mentioned in the Text

Blainley, G., *The Causes of War*, Free Press, 1973.

Boserup and Mack, *War and Weapons*, Pinter, 1974.

Booth and Wright, *American Thinking about Peace and War*, Harvester Press, 1978.

Burns, E. L. M., *Megamurder*, Harrap, 1966.

Burns, R. D., *Arms Control and Disarmament, A Bibliography*. ABC Clio, 1979.

Collins, J. M., *Imbalance of Power*, Presidio Press, 1978.

Benoit, Emile and Boulding, *Disarmament and the Economy*, 1963.

Cervenka and Rogers, *The Nuclear Axis*, Friedmann Books, 1978.

Cox, J., *Overkill*, Penguin, 1977.

Centre for Study of Developing Societies, *Disarmament, Development and a Just World Order*, New Delhi, 1978.

Eide and Thee, *Problems of Contemporary Militarism*, Croom-Helm, 1980.

Falk, R. A., and Mendlovitz, S. H., *The Strategy of World Order – Disarmament and Economic Development*, Praeger, 1966.

Gilpin, A. C., from *Foundation of Peace and Freedom*, Christopher Davies, 1975.

Hackett, J., *The Third World War, August 1985*, Sidgwick and Jackson, 1978.

Harbottle, M., *The Blue Berets*, Leo Cooper, 1971.

Jolly, Richard, *Disarmament and World Development*, 1978.

Joyce, J. A., *End of an Illusion*, Allen and Unwin, 1969.

Kaldor, M., *European Defence Industries*, Sussex Univ., 1972.

Kaldor, M., *World Military Order*, Macmillan, 1979.

Kennedy, G., *The Military in the Third World*, Duckworth, 1974.

Labour Party Defence Study Group, *Sense About Defence*, Quartet Books, 1977.

Lall, B. G., *Prosperity without Guns*, Cornell, 1978.

Lloyd and Sims, *British Writing on Disarmament*, Bibliography, Pinter, 1979.

SIPRI, *Military Research and Development*, Stockholm, 1972.

Thee, M., *Armaments and Disarmament in the Nuclear Age*, IPRI Stockholm, 1976.

Mitrany, D., *A Working Peace System*, Chicago, 1966.

Perlmutter, A., *The Military and Politics in Modern Times*, Yale, 1977.

Sampson, A., *The Arms Bazaar*, Coronet, 1978.

Sims, Nicholas A., *Approaches to Disarmament*, 1979.

Suter, Keith, *Uranium, the Law and You*, Friends of the Earth, 1978, Sydney, Australia.

United Nations and Disarmament Yearbook, Annual, 1978.

UN Documents

Economic and Social Consequences of the Armaments Race and its Extremely Harmful Effects on World Peace and Security (A/32/88 Rev. 1) (Sales Wo.: E 78.IX 1).

Report of Ad-Hoc Group of the Special Session on Disarmament on the Relationship between Disarmament and Development (A/S-10/9).

Final Document of the Special Session on Disarmament (1978).

Document of the General Assembly 33rd Session on Disarmament and Development (A/C.1/33/L.12/Rev.1).

Report of the Group of Governmental Experts on the Relationship between Disarmament and Development (A/33/317).

Document of the General Assembly, 34th Session: Relationship between Disarmament and Development (A/34/534).

ECOSOC: Committee for Development Planning – Disarmament and Development: An Analytical Survey (E/AC.54/L.90).

Disarmament and Science and Technology for Development (A/CONF.81/5/Add.2).

Reports and Studies

Arms Production and Employment in the Netherlands, Peace Research Centre, University of Nijmegen.

Asquith, Phil, *A Contribution to Disarmament and the Reduction of Social Conflict*, The Lucas Aerospace Corporate Plan, UK, 1979.

Ball, Nicole and Leitenberg, M., *Disarmament and Development*.

Scientific Symposium on 'Problems of the Conversion from War to Peace Production', Vienna , March–April 1979.

Emelyanov, Vasily, *Disarmament and Reconversion of the Defence Industry*.

Faramazyan, R. A., *Economic and Social Problems of Conversion*, Vienna, 1979.

Knorr, Lorenz, *The Political Aspect of Conversion from War to Peace Production*.

Leitenberg, M., *Defence Industry Conversion in the United States*; *USSR Economy, Defence Industry, and Military Expenditure*, Cornell Univ., 1979.

Lock, P., *Obstacles to Disarmament*, UNESCO Expert Meeting, Paris, 1978.

McNamara, Robert S., *Development and the Arms Race*.

März, Eduard, *The Impact of Military Expenditure on Economic Development*.

Rölling, B. V. A., *Disarmament and Development – Perspective of Security*.

SIPRI, *The Arms Trade with the Third World*, Penguin, 1974.

Soukup, Miroslav, *Principles of Establishing A Comprehensive Programme of Global Development*, Supplementary Resources Gained from Disarmament.

Värynen, Raimo, *Employment, Economic Policy and Military Production*, Tampere, 1979.

Wallensteen, P., *Experiences in Disarmament*, Conversion of Military Industry, Uppsala University, 1978.

Index

207

SALT II, 16, 31-2, 37, 42-3, 101
SALT III, 42-3
Sampson, Anthony, 108
— *The Arms Bazaar*, 108-9
Schlesinger, James, 90
Science, 71
Sense about Defence, x
Serxner, Dr Jonathan, 52
Shah of Iran, 107, 110, 112
Sidgwick and Jackson, publ., x
Siilasvuo, General Ensio, 166
Sivard, Ruth Leger, ix, 128
SLBMs, 29, 32
Smithsonian Institution, ix
Sokolovskii, Marshal, 82, 85
Staff College, Camberley, 64
Stennis, Senator John, 84
Stevenson, Adlai, 160
Suter, Dr Keith, 46
Swedish International Peace
  Research Institute, ix, 5, 49

Tankology, 68-72
Taylor, A. J. P., 53
Thatcher, Margaret, 2, 10, 11
Thermonuclear War, On, 15
Third World, 114-18
*Third World War, August 1985,
  The*, x, 74, 75, 151
Torrey Canyon, 3
Trade in arms, 104-6, 112-19
Treires, James, 127-8
Tueni, Ambassador, 64
Turkey, 140-145

UNESCO, 172-3
United Kingdom:
— British Army Equipment
  Exhibition, 103
— Defence White Paper (1980),
  136
— Ministry of Defence, 29-30
United Nations:
— Charter, 2
— Committee for Development
  Planning, 158
— Department of Public Infor-
  mation, x

— Emergency Force (UNEF),
  164-7
— Environment programme, 39
— Expert Group on Seismic
  Detection, 161
— General Assembly, 45
— — Policy speech by President
  Carter, 56
— Human Rights Commission, 7,
  174-5
— Interim Force in Lebanon
  (UNIFIL), 167-8
— Outer Space Committee, 162
— Peacekeeping Force in Cyprus,
  141
— Report by consultant experts
  on nuclear war (1968), 21-2,
  78
— Special sessions on disar-
  mament, x, 137, 154, 156, 159
— Truce Supervisory Service
  (Palestine), 15
United States:
— Armed Services Committee,
  84
— Arms Control and Disar-
  mament Agency, 180
— Congress, 157
— Defence budget, 35, 133
— National Science Foundation,
  160
— Office of Technology Assess-
  ment of Congress, 49
— State Department, ix, 29, 159
— — Bureau of Public Affairs,
  26
— Veterans' Appeals Board, 46
Uranium, 47, 50, 56

Vance, Cyrus, 100-101
Vickers Limited, 135

Wadlow, René, x, 62
Waldheim, Kurt,
Waldheim-Natural, Mrs L., x
Walker, Dr Alan, 181
Warnke, Paul, 125-6
WAPO, 10, 16, 44

210